Exploring Ethical Non-Monogamy

Practical Steps to Manage Fear, Improve Communication, Build Positive Relationships, & Increase Personal Growth (in the Polyamory & Open Lifestyle)

Amara & Samir Everbond

Contents

Personal Note from Amara Everbond

∞

Once upon a time, I believed in fairytales. True Love's Kiss, Prince Charming, and the Happily Ever After story. I was born into a Western society where Disney played over and over again and into a Christian family with strong beliefs in monogamy.

As a little girl, I connected love with the idea of finding a soulmate. My life's mission was to find "The One" and live out my own fairytale. What made my story even crazier was that I had no idea that anything other than monogamy existed. In my mind, monogamy was the natural and the only moral way to love and build partnerships.

Then I thought about how we have more than one child and love each of them in their unique ways, how we can have more than one pet and care for them all. Even though we can have multiple friends, each offering a distinct connection, we limit ourselves to one romantic partnership and deny ourselves the opportunity to connect to others in such a deep way.

The story shifted and evolved as I delved into the complexities of human history and the evolution of our relationship models. I stumbled upon a different narrative that challenged the idea of monogamy as the sole path to love. It was as if I had uncovered a hidden, forgotten chapter of our story.

This new story, rooted in anthropology and history, revealed that, while prevalent today, monogamy isn't the only way to structure relationships. It's not the only model that has existed throughout human history. Our ancestors, in a time before agriculture reshaped our lives, likely practiced non-monogamy as a norm.

The idea of multiple, flexible partnerships and fluid connections was prevalent among our hunter-gatherer ancestors. Small, nomadic groups and a lack of property ownership made rigid, monogamous relationships impractical. Instead, relationships were formed based on shared goals, emotional bonds, and practicality. It wasn't about strict exclusivity but about the ebb and flow of connections that best served the community and individuals involved.

It was only with the advent of agriculture and the concept of property ownership that monogamy became increasingly prominent. The shift towards settled communities required clear family lines for legal and social reasons, and monogamy served this purpose. Marriage contracts emerged as a way to preserve wealth and maintain social order.

Monogamy certainly works for many people as a relationship style. It is a choice that everyone has the right to make according to their beliefs, needs, and values. There is nothing wrong with it; if it makes you happy and fulfilled, monogamy deserves a place in your relationship paradigm. However, for Samir and I, and for many of our clients and friends that we have encountered along this journey, monogamy has led to more toxicity and issues than it has solved. The concept of Toxic Monogamy is a significant aspect of my personal journey that led me to embrace non-monogamy. It's a concept that delves into the unhealthy dynamics and expectations that can sometimes manifest within monogamous relationships. Let's explore this further.

Toxic Monogamy is a term used to describe the detrimental aspects of some monogamous relationships, which can include:

- **Unrealistic Expectations:** In many monogamous relationships, societal and personal expectations often lead to unrealistic ideals. We're conditioned to believe that a single person should fulfill all our emotional, physical, and social needs. One person is now responsible for being everything to their partner, leading to codependence and lack of autonomy, setting the stage for disappointment, as no person can be everything to us.

- **Possessiveness:** Traditional monogamy can sometimes foster possessiveness, where one partner feels a sense of ownership over the other. This possessiveness can lead to jealousy and control issues, ultimately harming the relationship.

- **Emotional Dependency:** Toxic Monogamy often perpetuates emotional dependency, where an individual's happiness solely relies on their partner. This kind of emotional codependency can result in an unhealthy, unbalanced dynamic.

My journey into non-monogamy became a spiritual awakening because it challenged these limiting beliefs and offered an alternative perspective. It was a process of breaking free from the constraints of Toxic Monogamy and embracing new, healthier belief systems. This transformation was liberating for me, my husband, and most of the other people we encountered.

Understanding this, I've come to appreciate the diversity of relationship models. Non-monogamy, whether in the form of polyamory, open relationships, or other variants, challenges the narrative that monogamy is the only valid or moral way to love. Monogamy is ONE way to love but not the ONLY way to love. It emphasizes open communication, consent, and mutual respect within the boundaries of consensual partnerships.

This journey allowed us to release ourselves from the barriers of Toxic Monogamy. It provided us with the tools to navigate relationships with authenticity and love within our partnership and as we supported our clients on their unique journeys toward healthier, more fulfilling relationships. It was a transformative path toward self-discovery and reimagining what love and connection mean in our lives.

It's important to clarify that in sharing this narrative and journey into non-monogamy, I am not advocating that non-monogamy is the "better" way of being in relationships. The intent of this book is not to persuade you to adopt non-monogamy as your relationship model. Instead, we invite you to be open-minded, to listen to a different tale than the one you grew up hearing throughout your life, and to remain curious. If, after exploring these ideas, you still choose monogamy as your preferred relationship style, that's okay. In fact, I am happy for you because you made that choice consciously and with intention. Most people have yet to choose their relationship style deliberately. Instead, they go with what their parents or society dictated. We encourage you to recognize that non-monogamy is another option, just as monogamy is a choice. You have the power to choose the way you wish to relate to others, free from the constraints of conditioning and indoctrination.

Perhaps, after reading this book, you decide to stay monogamous but without the toxic belief systems that can sometimes accompany it. The mere act of shedding these unhealthy notions is, in itself, a valuable reason to explore the contents of this book. Empower yourself to embrace a healthier, more authentic monogamy or, if you so choose, to consider the possibilities that come with non-monogamous relationships. Ultimately, it's about broadening our horizons and embracing the diversity of human connections and relationship choices, and that journey is worth every page turned.

I stand for a New Earth built on more love, boundless freedom, and open hearts. It's a world where everyone has the autonomy to define their values and shape their identity, free from judgment or the constraints of societal molds. This book serves as your invitation, an opportunity for each person to explore, question the established narrative, and embrace a life that is uniquely and profoundly fulfilling to you. Are you ready to dive in?

With love and an open heart,
Amara Everbond

Introduction

∞

Did you know that you probably know someone secretly dipping their toes into non-monogamy? According to Esquire Magazine, a recent study in the Journal of Sex and Marital Therapy surveyed 87,000 people and discovered that 20% of single people had tried a non-monogamous arrangement at some point.[1]

That means one in five people have said, "Hey, traditional monogamy, I need some space." It's estimated that five percent of Americans are non-monogamous.[2]

This figure could be inaccurate due to a lack of disclosure because there is still a lot of stigma attached to non-monogamy. Who knows how many more are hiding in the monogamous closet, afraid of societal judgment? Still, it is a subject that has gained increasing popularity and interest in recent years. So, you are not alone in your curiosity or desire to explore this subject. You may be one of those people or just curious about it, which led you here. Or maybe your partner planted the seed in your head, you saw it on a reality TV show, or your friend is living the lifestyle. Either way, we will help you explore and navigate the shores of *ethical* non-monogamy. Remember, if it's not consensual, it's not ethical—and unethical means you're veering into Cheaterville (but nobody wants to buy real estate there). So, from now on, when we say the word *non-monogamy*, we are referring to *ethical* or *consensual non-monogamy* (or *ENM* for short).

Love is not a one-size-fits-all thing. We are not *all* cut from the same cloth, and every person should be allowed to decide the relationship that works for them without feeling judged or shunned. We're here to say that love comes in more flavors than Baskin-Robbins ice cream, and everyone should have a scoop of their choosing without getting side-eyed.

Monogamy is common, yet not for everyone. We are not here to say monogamy is *bad* and non-monogamy is *good*. Instead, we want *you* to have the opportunity to decide what is right for *you*.

Suppose you feel that a traditional monogamous arrangement might not be your best choice. In that case, we will guide you in stepping into ENM (ethical non-monogamy, also called consensual non-monogamy) and help you understand a concept not taught in the Western world because of the societal norms surrounding relationships.

In its broadest sense, non-monogamy is a term used to describe any intimate relationship that involves more than two people. It encompasses numerous relationship styles, including polyamory, open relationships, and swinging. Non-monogamy challenges the traditional societal norms of monogamy and allows individuals to explore multiple connections and forms of love simultaneously.

Ethical non-monogamy is a relationship style in which everyone involved consents (this is the key word here) to any of them having multiple partners. There is a sense in non-monogamy that it's almost unfair to ask one person to be everything to another person without piling on unnecessary pressure. That old-fashioned notion of finding "the one" suggests humans can only love one person when we know this isn't true. Think about it: We love our family members, friends, children, and pets—and often many of them—but somehow, when it comes to romantic partners, we're assumed to be able to love only one person. Having several partners enables us to explore various experiences while fulfilling our needs and desires with different people. Non-monogamy involves learning to live with an open heart and not close ourselves off from the experiences and lessons the world offers us.

We've got your back as we tackle everything from breaking down myths and handling those anxiety-ridden moments to creating solid relationships that would make a relationship guru proud. We will give you practical advice, relatable examples, and a sense of community for those new to non-monogamy or seeking open discussions about it. You will develop personal growth and emotional intelligence for more positive relationships as we dispel the myths, manage any anxieties that prop up, and improve communication with your partner(s).

We are glad you are open to embracing a richer and more fulfilling life. You may be dipping your toe or have experienced feelings of uncertainty for a while, or you may need permission to give yourself the nudge to explore a different type of relationship. No matter what your reason, we are pleased that we can explore this journey together.

We hope to provide you with the necessary tools to find your way through this intricate and ultimately rewarding way of life. We welcome you to this voyage of self-discovery! You are not alone in this venture. More and more people are choosing to free themselves from a monogamous lifestyle to embrace the freedom of non-monogamy. There may be occasions when you need slightly more reassurance to navigate the more difficult times; we will support you in doing just that.

Our goal by the end of this book is to help you:

- Understand the myths, misconceptions, and different types of non-monogamy

- Appreciate why non-monogamy might be the right choice for you (or a choice in general for others)

- Develop practical tools to overcome jealousy, anxiety, and other negative emotions that might creep up

- Understand the importance of communication in non-monogamy

- Create boundaries and agreements that work for everyone involved

- Build trusting and positive relationships with one or more partners

- Navigate relationship transitions in non-monogamy

- Find personal growth through ENM

Throughout this book, we provide you with as much unbiased and non-judgmental guidance and insights as humanly possible. We use pen names (Amara & Samir are not our real names) because we like our privacy. The names of the people in the stories and examples throughout this book have also been changed to respect our client's privacy.

It's crucial to recognize that the spectrum of non-monogamous styles is vast and varied. While we strive to provide comprehensive advice, the sheer diversity of these relationship dynamics would make this book so massive it would make "War and Peace" look like a pamphlet. Therefore, we ask for your understanding if we can't delve into every nuance or variation that exists within relationships. Our intention is not to offend, but to acknowledge the limitations of language.

This book is crafted for those exploring ethical non-monogamy, especially couples with a history of monogamy seeking to embark on this journey together. It's an excellent book for beginners or those who have started but have yet to lay a foundation for a harmonious ENM lifestyle. For those who are more advanced and are picking up this book – you may contemplate the foundations we share or pass it along to a friend, family member, or partner who wants to understand more about this lifestyle or your relationship preferences. Many of our clients initially approach us with a desire to open up their relationship, and we often guide them through a more hierarchal framework initially for the sake of nervous system regulation. From there, they organically find their way into other forms that resonate with them.

In our experience, relationships can bring forth triggers, wounds, fears, insecurities, and limiting beliefs from the past. However, within a supportive partnership, these challenges can be transformed into opportunities for healing and growth, especially in the realm of ethical non-monogamy. This is the essence of our book—to support you in finding what works best for your most authentic and vibrant self.

Whether you're just starting your journey or have been navigating non-monogamy for a while, this book offers nuggets of wisdom that, upon reflection, can support your path. While what works for us and our ideal clients may not be a one-size-fits-all solution for you, there is still much to learn from these pages, regardless of your relationship style.

There is still a surprising amount of ignorance regarding this lifestyle choice, which can lead to non-monogamous individuals feeling isolated, judged, or completely misunderstood. So, in the first chapter, we will start by unveiling some of the common myths and misconceptions surrounding it. So, let the door to ENM swing open, and let's explore Chapter 1.

Non-monogamy Demystified

People have been subjected to prejudices and expectations since recorded history began:

- What they can and cannot do.

- What they should do.

- When they should do it.

- With whom they should do it.

Sadly, one area where this is especially true is the choice of partner.

Imagine if we actually followed all those social norms to the letter. We'd all be living in these cookie-cutter monogamous, opposite-sex marriages with exactly 1.94 children, a white picket fence, and a pet that never listens.[3]

Imagine if we actually followed all those social norms to the letter. We'd all be living in these cookie-cutter monogamous, opposite-sex marriages with exactly 1.94 children, a white picket fence, and a pet that never listens.[4] But thank goodness, life is messier than a toddler's attempt at finger painting. Just like we come in all different shapes and sizes, our needs, wants, desires, and fantasies are as diverse as a box of chocolates.

Before we sink our teeth into non-monogamy and all its hues, let's laugh at the myths and misconceptions that come with this adventurous lifestyle. Perhaps these misconceptions have been holding you back from exploring non-monogamy. Maybe you're curious about what non-monogamy entails and how it will fit into your current situation.

Worry not; we'll be covering everything you need to know, but for now, let's tackle some of those wacky myths and misconceptions related to non-monogamy to set your mind at ease.

The Many Faces of Non-monogamy

When most of us think about non-monogamy (consensual or ethical non-monogamy, of course), most people think of sex-crazed orgies or pleasure dens akin to those seen in *Game of Thrones*. Contrary to these beliefs, non-monogamy rarely delves into the world of orgies (unless the participants choose it).

The norms and dynamics of the people involved give non-monogamy various forms. From voyeurism to swinging, cohabitating to triads, there are more combinations than a Rubik's Cube on steroids. Research has found that 1 in 5 people engage in non-monogamy.[5]

These are the most common non-monogamous relationships:

- **Swinging** involves established couples (often married) who like to spice things up by engaging in playful and adventurous sexual activities with other pairs.

- **Polyamory** allows each person in the relationship to have outside relationships with the consent and knowledge of all parties. Often, polyamorous relationships have two or more people in the primary relationship who live and play together.

- **Polyfidelity** is polyamory's cool cousin. It involves three or more people in a relationship, but here is the twist: They do not explore relationships outside of their love bubble. A common type of polyfidelity is a throuple.

- **Polygamy** (not to be confused with polyamory) typically involves one person (let us call them

Sam) having multiple partners; however, the partners only have a relationship with Sam. In polygamy, "Sam" can be any gender, as can the partners. **Polygyny**, the most common type of polygamy, is what most people think of when thinking about polygamy, where one man takes on many wives.

- **Open relationships** involve a couple agreeing to engage in relationships with others. These relationships do not typically include both parties in the couple. Outside relationships may involve emotional, sexual, or romantic elements. However, it is understood that the primary partner always takes precedence over all other partnerships. External relationships can be short- or long-term, depending on the agreement.

- **Monogamish relationships** involve a primarily monogamous couple that allows sexual contact (in varying degrees) with others. Rules can include anything from limitations on the type of sexual activity to location or time. Casual dating and casual sex are two of the most common monogamish setups.

- **Relationship Anarchy** (despite its name) is all about each partner being equal. People in this type of non-monogamy don't play favorites; no one partner gets more attention than another. Relationship anarchy is centered on autonomy and freedom; no relationship hierarchies are allowed. Forget about the labels and categories; it doesn't matter if the relationships are romantic, platonic, or sexual; they are what they are, and each one is just as important as the others.

But remember, it's not a love free-for-all; it's all based on trust, honesty, and consent. Non-monogamy isn't a sneaky way to cheat on your partner; it's more like a love party where everyone's invited, and the VIP guest list can be meticulously managed.

Before entering a non-monogamous situation, you and your partner will establish the ground rules. These are the hard no's, the limits to what you can and can't do, and where your boundaries are.

These ground rules can change over time; remember that these changes should always be discussed long before playtime. Changes should never be made in the heat of the moment. Discuss changes, get consent, and avoid those awkward "oops" moments.

Remember, these ground rules are as unique as your fingerprint. From "no singing in the shower with others" to "your leftover tacos are only for secondary partners on Tuesdays," it's all about what works for you and your partners. These discussions create a safe, transparent, and respectful love playground. It's like building a cozy blanket fort where you and your partner(s) can embark on thrilling adventures without any worries. We'll cover more about ground rules in Chapter 6.

But, before diving deeper into the ground rules world, let's tackle some common misconceptions about ENM.

Debunking Misconceptions About Non-monogamy

With all the misconceptions surrounding non-monogamy, it is often misunderstood. It's like a game of telephone, but with relationships. People often get the wrong idea, but let's set the record straight! Below, we'll debunk eight of ENM's central myths and misconceptions.

Myth #1: Non-monogamy Goes Against Our Human Nature

The belief that non-monogamy is unnatural or that human beings are made to be monogamous is a societal norm. Still, many experts and scientists argue that our species is not monogamous by nature but by nurture.

It's estimated that around 70% of people in monogamous marriages cheat at least once during their marriage, and up to 40% of monogamous relationships (unmarried) experience at least one instance of cheating.[6] These numbers tell us that monogamy may not be the best option for everyone.

In their book *Sex at Dawn: The Prehistoric Origins of Modern Sexuality*, authors Christopher Ryan and Cacilda Jethá state that today's societal "norms" are not aligned with our biological evolutionary history, and as humans, we are inherently (and historically) non-monogamous.

There are numerous examples of this throughout our species' history. The Mosuo people are known for their practice of "walking marriages," where individuals have the freedom to form multiple romantic and sexual partnerships throughout their lives. In ancient Rome, both men and women engaged in extramarital affairs with the premise that they would not jeopardize the sanctity of their marriage or family life. Polyandry was practiced by the Maasai people in pre-colonial Africa, which meant that a woman would have numerous spouses, generally brothers. Polygyny was practiced by the Ashanti of Ghana, in which a man had multiple wives. The Celts' sexual behavior was quite open and free, with both men and women engaging with several partners. In fact, monogamy is a social construct that has been imposed on us for roughly 1,000 years.[7] This is only a blimp of time in human history, so it's more logical to say that monogamy is relatively new and abnormal if you look at our evolutionary timeline.

As humans, we evolved within tribes and groups that shared everything—food, shelter, child care, protection, and sexual partners. That leads most of us to ask, "What has changed?" We went from a tribe mentality where all the males got food for the entire group to an agriculturalist paradigm where one man owns acres of land and wants to pass it on to their biological child, not another man's. They needed a wife who would bear their children, not someone else's. Monogamy is a patriarchal construct where having one's own child (versus a tribe-parented child) was a big deal to ensure there was an heir to inherit the wealth. Sadly, we often allow societal and cultural norms to influence us more than our biological nature. A nuclear family's "normal" life has led to humans suppressing their natural inclinations, including non-monogamy.[8]

With the amount of collapsed families, cheating, and division in marriages in today's day, this is anything but "normal." The authors of *Sex at Dawn* also believe that the shift towards monogamy as a norm has created many psychological and societal struggles. They state that accepting non-monogamy as a viable option—not better or worse than monogamy, but just as valid—could allow for healthier, happier, and more fulfilling relationships.

Studies done over the years have found that most people want various types of partners, both romantically and sexually.[9] Many people who engage in ENM report that the lifestyle allows them to pursue a life that's true to who they are and what they want.

Myth #2: Once Ground Rules Are in Place, They Can't Be Changed

As we learn, grow, and change, so do our boundaries and limits. The ground rules you start with may differ from those that stay in place over the years. So let your partner know what makes you feel warm and fuzzy and what makes you go, "Uh-uh, nope, no way!" It's all about finding that sweet spot where everyone feels happy and respected in each moment.

As your feelings or circumstances change, so can the rules. Each person in the relationship should express their comfort levels, feelings, and boundaries. In ENM, it's all about feeling safe and comfortable. And if that safety blanket starts feeling more like a straitjacket, it's time to speak up. Respectful, ethical, non-monogamous situations allow for this change.

Myth #3: Non-monogamous People Are Scared of Commitment

Another common misconception is that non-monogamous people are scared of or can't commit. This isn't the case at all. What commitment looks like to you will look different to others, and this is true for non-monogamous relationships, too.

In the case of a polyamorous relationship, the individuals involved show trust, respect, love, dedication, and responsibility to multiple people at once. By maintaining those relationships, they're showing commitment to numerous people. So, calling non-monogamous folks commitment-phobic is like saying pineapples don't belong on pizza. It's just not true. It may look different from what it looks like in a monogamous relationship. Still, commitment is what makes an ENM relationship possible. Without the commitment to your partner(s), you are someone who sleeps around or has sex with anyone. To be able to spend time, share experiences, and transfer sexual energy with someone else but still love, give, care, and provide for your partner is what makes non-monogamous people's commitment that much stronger. The most robust relationships are those who stay committed to each other no matter what they do or who they interact with.

Myth #4: Non-monogamy Is an Excuse to Sleep Around or Cheat

There's a Grand Canyon-sized chasm between cheating and non-monogamy. Cheating is like sneaking into a cookie jar when your mom says, "Hands off!" You're going behind someone's back and breaking their trust. In contrast, there's no "Mission Impossible" secrecy in non-monogamy. Everything is done consensually and with clear communication, respect, and honesty.

In non-monogamous relationships, everyone knows the arrangement and agrees to the ground rules. 43 - 56% of people in non-monogamous relationships state that they feel more security, honesty, and trust in their non-monogamous relationship than they did in a monogamous relationship.[10]

For instance, Janey and Sean have been married for six years and have been in a non-monogamous relationship since they got together. Being in a polyamorous relationship allows them to express everything to each other - their excitement, fears, desires, and needs without fear of judgment or being shut down. If they can't fulfill the needs each of them has, they can find it outside the relationship in a respectful, agreed-upon way. They don't feel the need to cheat (and violate the trust they've developed) because they've established ground rules that everyone follows to keep everyone on the same page.

Myth #5: Non-monogamy Is All About the Sex

There are countless reasons why someone might choose non-monogamy. Sure, sex and all its acrobatics can be part of the equation. Still, non-monogamy is about forming and exploring meaningful connections with people – without sneaking around like an outlaw.

For example, although a polyamorous relationship includes multiple people, each pairing will form deep emotional bonds with each other that are shared between them alone. Most people who choose non-monogamy do so for reasons other than *just* sex, such as connection, understanding, and a shared experience.

Just look at Leila; she's living the polyamorous dream. She has the safety and consistency of her primary relationship with Aaron and Senna (who do not have relationships outside the throuple). Still, she can explore her other interests (Leila identifies as pansexual) with secondary partners. She finds a lot of connection in the shared experience of doing nude paintings with her partner, Patrick. Their relationship has never become fully sexual, but they enjoy visually exploring each other's bodies.

Myth #6: Non-monogamy Is Selfish

ENM isn't a one-sided affair where one person gets all the benefits while leaving others high and dry. In ethical and consensual non-monogamous relationships, all parties are fully aware of and content with the rules and arrangement. It's about multiple people making choices and consent, not just one person (we call that a dictator).

The magic happens when folks decide that sharing is caring (like how we were taught in preschool). It's not about selfishness but the willingness to share affection, emotional connections, and even physical intimacy with others. In a way, it's a demonstration of generosity and openness rather than self-centeredness. The aim is not to monopolize affection but to expand the horizons of love and relationships.

Additionally, many people in non-monogamous relationships say that their lifestyle experience has strengthened their primary relationship and helped them better solve issues and communicate.[11] When all parties are authentically open and honest about their needs and boundaries, it can lead to more effective communication and conflict resolution. This doesn't sound like selfishness; it sounds like the recipe for healthier relationships.

Myth #7: Non-monogamy Is Only for Young People

Non-monogamy doesn't come with an age limit, just like love doesn't ask for your ID before it sweeps you off your feet. It also does not come with gender or sexual orientation limits. Non-monogamy is available for all to enjoy in their own way and time.

Meet Andy, a 53-year-old who has been in a relationship with 44-year-old Colleen for seven years. They've been enjoying a mono/poly relationship since they got together. Since Colleen is bisexual, she engages in casual sex with other women. Still, Andy is only in a relationship with Colleen. He is happy that she is happy, and since he feels secure in himself, he does not feel jealous or inadequate if she is with someone who isn't him. They both are perfectly content with their arrangement.

Whether you're in your roaring 20s, fabulous 40s, or sensational 60s, straight, bisexual, pansexual, single, married, dating, or anything in between, non-monogamy doesn't discriminate. It's all about what tickles your fancy (and who tickles it with your consent).

Myth #8: People Only Seek Non-monogamy When Their Relationship's Failing

When couples engage in non-monogamy, many assume it's because the relationship is failing or the individuals in the pair are lonely or dissatisfied. Let's clarify: Non-monogamy is not a Band-Aid to solve your relationship's problems.

According to New York-based psychotherapist Rebecca Sokoll, trying to fix your relationship with non-monogamy is about as effective as having a baby do the same thing - it doesn't work. She says, "You need a strong and healthy relationship to transition to non-mo nogamy."[12]

It is strongly recommended that you never engage in non-monogamy to put more distance between yourself and your primary spouse. Hanna Zipes Basal, a Minnesota-based non-monogamy psychotherapist, says, "Couples succeed when they enter non-monogamy with an already secure functioning relationship when they both equally desire non-monogamy and have done their hom ework."[13]

Many people in non-monogamous relationships state that they're delighted in their primary relationships and that non-monogamy is a way of improving that further, not a way of saving the relationship. Many couples we met who used ENM to fix their relationship are no longer together. Only the ones doing it to enhance their relationship (and not save it) stuck it out long term.

What Does This All Mean?

At the end of the day, non-monogamy is gaining attention and popularity. Still, that doesn't mean it comes without stigma, stereotypes, and misconceptions. We've looked at some of the foremost myths surrounding this lifestyle.

The main things to understand about non-monogamy are:

- It's completely natural (whereas monogamy is how we are raised and conditioned by society, church, and Hollywood).

- There's a lot of freedom: rules can change at any time.

- Non-monogamists don't fear commitment.

- Non-monogamists want to give and receive more love in their lives; it's got nothing to do with cheating.

- It's about connection and intimacy (not only about sex).

- It's inclusive - there's nothing selfish about it.

- It's for anyone and everyone - young, elderly, single, married, and everything in between.

- It helps develop stronger bonds and commitment, but it is not a means to an end for failing relationships.

Non-monogamy involves communication, trust, consent, honesty, and exploration. However, non-monogamy isn't for everyone, and that's okay! The beauty of life is that we all get to choose what type of relationship works best for us and our needs.

Society may have its own rulebook, but guess what? You don't have to follow it! If you're interested in or are considering non-monogamy, that's great! Be your fabulous, unique self, and let society scratch its head in confusion as you join along for the ride!

Navigating Society's Reaction to Non-Monogamy

As society evolves, so will our understanding of love, affection, sex, and relationships. Non-monogamy was once standard, but it seems like a foreign concept today. "How dare you love more than one person!" they might say. Poking the proverbial bear and shaking things up is frowned upon, and we're encouraged to swim with the current and conform to norms.

Yet "normal" doesn't make it "right," and you can express yourself and experiment however you choose. Suppose you're in a non-monogamous relationship (or are considering exploring the lifestyle). In that case, you may be experiencing or are worried about facing discrimination, disrespect, and judgment. Don't you love it when people make you feel wrong about your beliefs and lifestyle choices?

Society can be harsh and cruel about things they don't understand. Here are a few ways you can handle this.

Have a Prepared Response

Suppose you're worried about facing any untoward or not-so-friendly reaction. In that case, it's helpful to have a prepared witty response or clever answer to the comments or questions you may receive.

Suppose Aunt Nosey decides to play detective about your love life at the next family gathering, and you're asked why you're non-monogamous. In that case, you can say, "Loving more than one person means more love is shared, and this world could use more love, not less," or say something like, "I value connection, authenticity, and unconditional love, so I have found this type of relationship style works best to support those values."

She'll be too busy deciphering your response to ask more questions.

Don't Say Anything

If you're worried about judgment, criticism, or emotional or physical danger. In that case, you can opt for stealth mode and choose not to say anything.

No rule says you need to tell anyone else your relationship status. It's much like asking about your sexual preferences – it's none of their business! Asking about someone's relationship - and worse, having an opinion about it - should be off-limits. If you don't want to answer, say so. Plead the fifth! If it is your truth, it needs no defense. "Everything that needs defense you do not want, for anything that needs defense will weaken you."[14] "Love rests in certainty. Only uncertainty can be defensive."[15]

Find a Support Network

Even if you choose to keep your relationship(s) secret, it's still helpful for good mental health to find a support network or community of non-monogamous people. You can do this in person, through social media like Facebook groups and Reddit threads (r/nonmonogamy is one of the most popular), or online via support websites like meetup.com.

The friends and confidantes you meet can offer emotional support, guidance, advice, and a safe place to share your challenges, fears, and experiences.

New to ENM, Erin became a secondary partner to a married couple recently. She wasn't sure whether she wanted to be in a throuple or a larger polyamorous group. Through Facebook, Erin connected with a few people, and they helped her explore her desires, fears, and interests. One of her friends suggested Erin meet with a polyamorous group first and see if she felt overwhelmed or excited by the situation. As it turned out, Erin joined that polyamorous group with four others and has been with them ever since. Without the advice, suggestions, and support of those she met online, Erin may still be wondering what to do and would have missed out on the experience she's now having.

So, now that we've dispelled some of the myths and misconceptions that come with non-monogamy and looked at how to navigate society's reaction to the lifestyle let's consider why people choose non-monogamy and why it could be a choice for you.

The Freedom of Choice: Embracing Relationship Diversity

In the same way that there are many reasons why you choose your partner(s), there are countless reasons why you may select non-monogamy. These reasons can include anything from exploring your sexuality to wanting variety (it *is* the spice of life, after all).

We will look at the *why* behind ENM and some of the reasons why people choose this path. Some of these may resonate with you, allowing you to know you're not "weird" or "strange" for wanting to explore this lifestyle. Let's check them out!

Non-monogamy as a Conscious Decision

For most people, non-monogamy isn't a given; it's an active choice. Those who choose a non-monogamous relationship typically do so because they find that monogamy doesn't fit with their needs, desires, and values.

No one slipped on a banana peel and fell into non-monogamy; it's a consciously chosen decision. Since it is a conscious decision, it reinforces that we are all autonomous in our relationships and can choose what works for us. This forms the cornerstone for building equal, respectful, and honest relationships.

Here are some of the most common reasons people choose non-monogamy:

Flexibility and Freedom

Non-monogamy allows you to explore intimate connections with various people. This offers a wider intellectual, sexual, and emotional landscape for all parties. You can find plenty of online forums and threads (such as the "nonmonogamy" thread on Reddit, "r/nonmonogamy") talking about the flexibility and freedom non-monogamy offers, making it a big plus for many in the community.

Sexual Exploration

Exploring our sexuality—our wants, needs, desires, and fantasies—is as natural and normal as breathing (and way more exciting). The thing is, your current partner may not be interested in exploring your specific interests. For some people, having a single partner at a time can be a tad confining and make them feel like they can't fully explore their sexuality. Non-monogamy allows people to explore their sexuality while still maintaining their current relationship.

James, for instance, is in a polyamorous relationship and enjoys a bit of rough foreplay, but his wife, Ami, doesn't want to participate in these acts. James explores this side of his desires with his lover, Jean, who gets a lot of pleasure from spanking and pinching James.

Have Variety

Since variety is the spice of life in non-monogamous relationships, this is undoubtedly the case. People who choose ENM want variety in their romantic and sexual relationships, and this lifestyle allows them to do so while enjoying a healthy relationship with their partner(s).

Sexually, this may mean they want to explore threesomes, same-sex intercourse, voyeurism, multiple partners, or anything else that tickles their fancy; they can fulfill their desires if all parties give a resounding "yes." Emotionally, it could be a want for extra cuddles, someone to wear "I'm with him" and "I'm with her" shirts, someone to sing with, or someone that loves an activity like camping, while your primary partner would prefer everything except that. Again, it's all about consent-filled fun.

More Love

The heart wants what it wants; sometimes, it wants more than just one! Is it crazy to believe you could love more than one person at a time? Some people may love multiple people simultaneously, making ENM an excellent choice. They won't be forced to choose a single partner but can explore their connection and love with various partners. They can also enjoy being loved by multiple people—the more, the merrier!

Others may want to open their hearts and minds to new possibilities. They love their current partner but do not want to close themselves off to the rest of the world. Maybe they enjoyed the dating scene, had fun swiping right, and didn't want to give up flirting with new people and the connections it can bring just because they found someone to spend their life with. Why not spread the love to more than one person? Who decreed that all other doors must be sealed shut upon finding one love? Oh, that's right, we don't have to! In this tale of love, there's no need for a "closed" sign on the front door.

Meet Needs

The biggest downside of a monogamous relationship is that one partner may not be able to meet the needs of the other. These needs can be physical, emotional, sexual, mental, or spiritual. Non-monogamy allows each partner to find others who meet their needs. You see, one partner might be your go-to for deep conversations, another might be your designated adventure buddy, and someone else might be your cuddle and reality TV partner.

This was the case for Jeremy and Stacie, who have been happily married for eight years. Around five years into their marriage, Jeremy started feeling stifled by the monogamous relationship; he was keen to explore different sexual positions and situations that Stacie wasn't interested in. Likewise, Stacie felt sad about having some of her emotional needs never met by Jeremy. She wanted someone who enjoyed cuddling on the couch and watching sappy reality TV shows, and that just wasn't Jeremy's thing. On the verge of cheating, Jeremy expressed his frustrations and desires to Stacie, deciding to be open and honest with her instead. This opened the door for Stacie to confess her frustrations, too. They agreed that they would find a joint partner willing to provide for their needs, and they opened their marriage to Samantha. Samantha spends two nights per week with them and the rest of the time with her husband, who spends his nights away from Samantha with his lover, Neil. All five people in this situation can safely, honestly, and respectfully explore their wants, needs, and desires.

It could be the need for companionship, someone to stimulate your intellect, or a thirst for adventure that one partner alone can't quench. By embracing non-monogamy, individuals can explore different connections and experiences to enhance their well-being and personal growth. It allows for a more holistic approach to relationships, where each person's needs are acknowledged and fulfilled to promote mutual happiness and fulfillment.

Unveiling Individual Motivations: Beyond the Stereotypes

Some people choose non-monogamy because it aligns better with their values or philosophical beliefs, whereas others prefer the lifestyle to explore their sexual desires and needs.[16]

Let's explore a few of the individual motivations why someone may choose non-monogamy.

Self-expression and Identity

Some people explore an ENM lifestyle as part of their self-expression and identity. For instance, someone who identifies as polyamorous can simultaneously enjoy relationships with multiple people. Being in a non-monogamous situation allows them to express themselves and their identity entirely.

Community

Participants in a recent study stated that non-monogamous relationships allowed them to join or build communities, friendships, and families in ways that made sense to them. Non-monogamy allowed them to pursue relationships aligned with their ethics and find like-minded individuals without hiding from their primary partner.[17]

Pragmatism

Many people who choose non-monogamous relationships find it a practical way to achieve their goals and manage their lives. Non-monogamy allows people to pursue relationships that suit their lives at any given moment.

Sarah has a monogamish relationship with her girlfriend, Jess. Sarah travels a lot for work, only spending two nights a week at home. While away, she has one-night stands and meet-ups with people she meets in the places she travels. But when she's home, she's all about quality time with Jess, her main squeeze.

Beliefs

Some non-monogamous enthusiasts think monogamy is like trying to fit into jeans two sizes too small — restrictive and potentially uncomfortable. Individuals in non-monogamous relationships can express their sexuality, emotions, and other aspects of their identities in a safe, accepting setting (no matter their jeans size). This leads to feelings of fulfillment, happiness, and contentment.

Personal Growth

Non-monogamous relationships can be an exciting and enlightening path to self-discovery and personal growth. It challenges those involved to confront their possessiveness, jealousy, and insecurities. You can emerge from the experience with more self-awareness, authenticity, and emotional resilience. It's a personal growth boot camp with extra cuddles.

Based on our monogamous upbringings, Disney movies, and parental conditioning, this was our most difficult challenge in attempting this lifestyle. We'd get jealous and suspicious if we saw each other around an attractive person because we felt insecure or inadequate. ENM provided us with relief from these feelings of ownership and possession, allowing us to feel secure in the knowledge that who our partner spends time with does not impact our worth or value as a person.

A study found that people in non-monogamous relationships experienced more personal growth than their monogamous counterparts.[18]

ENM also helps develop self-awareness and authenticity by articulating your wants, needs, emotions, and boundaries. An anonymous user on Quora's non-monogamy community shared that they've become more communicative, understanding, and self-aware since being in a polyamorous relationship. Another user said non-monogamy helped them cultivate honesty, acceptance, and empathy.

Pushing the boundaries of what society dictates to be "normal" can lead to a more profound understanding of who you are and what you want while living authentically, communicating honestly, and loving openly. Non-monogamy allows participants to expand and grow their relationship from a place of respect and security. When all your needs and wants are met, you can develop deeper connections and intimacy in your relationships and with yourself.

What Is The Reason for Your Relationship Model?

When you look at why you've chosen monogamy until now, you'll realize it wasn't a choice in most cases. Most of us are raised in a family, church, schooling system, or neighborhood where monogamy is the only option - other ways of relating are not discussed or presented, and if they are, it's in an off-limits kind of way. They tell you, "Don't do it; it's wrong."

In today's modern, connected world, where information is easy to find, we know many other types of relationships outside of monogamy. This means you now have a choice: what kind of relationship suits your needs?

Ask yourself a few questions on the journey from monogamy to non-monogamy. These will help you along your journey and determine whether ENM suits you.

Questions to consider:

- What types of relationships have you been in before?

- Why have you chosen these relationship types?

- Why did you decide to read this book?

- Is your partner(s) interested in non-monogamy?

- What are the reasons you're interested in learning more about ENM?

Now it's time to wear your detective hat and peek at your answers. Are you a one-partner kind of person, or is the non-monogamy path calling your name? If you feel the call, write down the reason why. Keep these answers somewhere safe so you can revisit them in moments of doubt.

At the end of the day, you need to explore what works best for *you*. There is no need to stress about finding the "perfect" answer. It's all about what floats your boat, tickles your fancy, and makes you dance happily. So, pick the option that aligns with your desires, needs, and values. The most vital aspect is prioritizing mutual consent and open communication in whatever relationship structure you choose - this will ensure all participants feel fulfilled and respected.

Once everyone involved is on the same page, you'll need to learn how to navigate the emotional rapids of jealousy and anxiety that come with non-monogamy, which we'll cover next.

Taming Jealousy and Anxiety

∞

For many people, the concept of an open relationship may seem simple in theory, yet many find it challenging to implement. We know that society has programmed us to believe that non-monogamy is just a fancy way to describe being unfaithful (ugh!). And don't even get me started on the moral police, who think having more than one partner is as wrong as believing the Earth is the center of the solar system. Even when all parties involved are consensual regarding the move to ethical non-monogamy, jealousy and anxiety might still sneak up on you like a mischievous little gremlin.

While you may have no issues exploring your sexual and emotional desires with others, it may be a different story when you acknowledge that your partner is doing the same thing. Suddenly, you may find yourself contemplating the meaning of life, the universe, and whether or not you left the stove on.

Despite what movies make us think about non-monogamy, it's not a bunch of people living together in a shared house, moving from one bed to the next in hours-long sex marathons (not that it can't be, if you want that). Non-monogamy takes some planning, a lot of conversing, and even more understanding and patience than waiting for your favorite TV show to return from a cliffhanger. Even couples navigating this lifestyle must overcome many hurdles with their primary and secondary partners. However, help is at hand if you want to understand the emotional landscape of non-monogamy. We'll look at the causes of jealousy and anxiety and discuss practical tools for managing these sneaky emotions.

The Unlearning Process

We've been programmed for monogamy, and breaking free from that programming is like switching from cable TV to streaming – it's a process, but it's worth it!

To flip this switch, we must do a lot of unlearning – of everything we've been told throughout our lives. For example, you may have considered how exciting it would be to have your pick of other partners but can't make the mental or physical leap from fantasy to reality.

From a very young age, we're introduced to the fairytale lifestyle of a prince saving a princess, getting married, popping out some adorable offspring, and living happily ever after. We've been so brainwashed with this concept of forsaking all others that we consider it a personal failure if we cannot sustain a relationship with our perceived idea of 'the one.'

This belief in all-encompassing exclusivity can become so deeply ingrained that jealousy can become an issue. One member of the polyamorous community said that, before exploring non-monogamy, they used to feel panicked when they discovered texts or emails from their partner to other people.[19] We have forgotten the "sharing is caring" mantra we learned as children regarding our partners; it was (obviously) only a motto for our beloved toys and candy but nothing else.

Relationships should feel safe, calm, exciting, and happy. If you feel like going up the creek without a paddle when your partner engages with others, a non-monogamous relationship may be the method of personal growth you need. But it all starts with unlearning.

To begin the unlearning process, you must challenge societal norms with the determination of a knight slaying dragons. You've got to question your beliefs about love, commitment, and possessiveness. It's time to break free from the chains of monogamy and create a life as authentic as a Picasso painting – weird and beautiful.

Let's cue in Jason and Louise, who were raised in strictly monogamous, Christian homes. A few years into their marriage, Jason confessed to Louise that he was always interested in what it would be like to be with another guy but that his religious background had made him shun that side of him, and he was tired of hiding his desire. With their backgrounds, they were both initially very resistant. Jason expressed his love for Louise and explained he didn't want to leave her but wanted to learn more about this side of him with her permission. After this conversation, they found Avril, who became a respected metamour to Louise and a great lover to Jason. It was initially a bit rocky, with Louise and Jason feeling guilt, doubt, and fear that they had to work through together and alone. They both needed time to self-reflect and decide what was important to them, not what society or religion says is correct. All three people created agreements and rules that evolved over time, ensuring they feel safe, prioritized, and respected while working through their emotions all together.

"One of the best practices you can have is a practice of self-reflection and unlearning," says Rachel Wright, a licensed psychotherapist.[20] She believes we are programmed for monogamy in this society, and even when choosing to practice a different lifestyle, the feelings and impulses we get don't always follow suit. After decades of society's morals and values being forced upon us, it's a significant transition to a non-monogamous mindset.

Transitioning from monogamy to non-monogamy takes time, and some days will be easier than others. Those in the non-monogamy community describe non-monogamy as a complex but worthy path—anything worth doing or having takes effort, practice, and time.

The Emotional Rollercoaster: Understanding the Impact of Non-monogamy on Mental Health

Non-monogamy can provoke a range of both positive and negative emotions. Anxiety and jealousy are experienced in most relationships at some point; however, these emotions can move up a notch in non-monogamous relationships.

At a fundamental level, there may be a fear of the societal viewpoint of the choice to have several partners. Although we have come a long way in accepting that relationships come in many different forms, some folks can't shake the idea that a monogamous relationship between a man and a woman is the norm. But hey, we'll keep spreading the love until everyone realizes that love can't be put in a box and labeled the same for everyone.

While non-monogamy can give participants freedom and empowerment, it does not come without challenges. The thrill of new relationships, known as New Relationship Energy (NRE), can lead to euphoria but may also create feelings of neglect in other partners. Many people struggle with thinking about their partner having a sexual or romantic relationship with others and may feel resentful, jealous, or fearful of rejection or abandonment. This is a normal human reaction that comes from the conditioning of monogamy.

The key to overcoming jealousy, rivalry, and insecurity comes from accepting that you are worthy of love regardless of your attributes and that no one can be more like you than you. Aubrey Marcus, a fitness expert and podcast host who has been very vocal about his open relationship lifestyle, explains that it is tough to get to this stage of belief, but only when you establish peace with yourself can you begin to practice compersion.[21]

Compersion is the enjoyment of someone else's enjoyment-it's like being the ultimate cheerleader for your partner's joy. This isn't the same as cuckolding, where you get sexual pleasure from the fantasy of your lover having sex with someone else. This is emotional pleasure, derived simply from their pleasure (be it sexual or not). It is the basis of real love. If you love someone, you are happy when they laugh, even when it isn't your joke.[22]

If your relationship has primary and secondary partners, you may become anxious that one of your partner's secondary partners will become more important than you. You may find yourself comparing what you have with your partner to their relationship with their other lovers. Personal insecurities may become highlighted, and the fear of abandonment may increase. Take a deep (very deep!) breath and see this as an opportunity to work on yourself, your insecurities, and your fears like Paul and Sophie have.

Paul and Sophie are primary (unmarried) partners and have been together for almost a decade. They both had experience with non-monogamy before meeting each other through a mutual friend. Neither had been in a serious relationship before, had been secondary partners, and had had one-night stands back then. They both felt anxiety and fear when they got together and realized how much they loved each other and wanted to commit long-term. However, Sophie worried that Paul would find another partner he preferred. She communicated this with Paul, who reassured her through regular check-ins and clear boundaries and rules. Sophie also saw her psychotherapist, who shed light on the root causes of her insecurities and fears of abandonment. Her parents divorced when she was young, and it always felt like her mom chose her new husband over her and her brother's needs. After recognizing that this is not the situation with Paul, she could keep her fears and worries at bay and explore her desires without fear of abandonment constantly peeping its ugly head.

In non-monogamous relationships, it's imperative that all partners, whether primary or secondary, are treated with equal respect and consideration. When someone initially enters a relationship as a secondary partner, they may grapple with feelings of hierarchy and question their role in the dynamic. They might long for emotional connection and affection without feeling limited to the convenience of the primary couple. However, it's crucial to recognize that each person in the relationship brings something valuable and unique to the dynamic. The focus should be on nurturing the emotional and mental well-being of everyone involved rather than rigid hierarchies. Suppose at any point the mental health of any partner, primary or secondary, is compromised. In that case, it serves as a signal to reassess the relationship dynamics and engage in compassionate conversations with all parties. These discussions should aim to ensure that each partner's needs are acknowledged, that there is a sense of belonging, and that everyone feels like an integral part of the broader relationship. The overarching goal is to create a space where everyone's well-being is safeguarded and where each person is treated with the respect, love, and care they deserve.

Even though this lifestyle choice requires some planning to allow things to go smoothly, many couples rise above the initial distress and experience increased pleasure and enjoyment. Open-hearted living improves their ability to communicate honestly with their partner and allows their authenticity to shine through.

For many, adopting this lifestyle is born out of a collective consciousness with their partner(s).

Stephanie, who lives a polyamorous lifestyle with her husband, stated, "I didn't go through this mission alone, either; this was a partnership exploring a new way of living, one that had the potential to be rich and fulfilling. We stayed up late, talking for hours about what we would want, the rules (trust me, there are many), vetoes and breaks, age limits, and sleeping over. This all came from a place of deep love and commitment, which might sound counterintuitive, but to open up a marriage, it's vital."[23]

Unpacking the Fear: Understanding the Root Cause of Anxiety in Non-monogamy

As society dictates that monogamy is the only valid relationship style, many people struggle with an internal conflict between "right" and "wrong" when considering a non-monogamous life. "Abandonment anxiety," the fear of a loved one leaving us, can worsen this anxiety. It's a fear we all have (thanks, brain!), but that doesn't make it any easier, especially in non-monogamy.

The wonderful thing about non-monogamy is that it eliminates the need to worry about being abandoned. Non-monogamy allows for exploring multiple connections and relationships, which can provide a sense of security and reassurance. By embracing the idea that love is not limited or exclusive, individuals in non-monogamous relationships can find comfort in knowing that their partner's love for someone else does not diminish their worth or place in their partner's life. This shift in perspective can help alleviate abandonment anxiety and foster a more inclusive and accepting approach to love and relationships.

If you ask anyone who's been living this lifestyle for a while, they'll tell you they had the same fears and worries. You're swimming against the current in a river full of social norms, but that doesn't mean you're swimming the wrong way; it just means you're choosing a different way to enjoy and explore your needs and wants.

Understanding why you feel anxious, and the root causes behind these feelings are the first step to easing your fears. Recognizing the potentially negative impact that society has had on your belief systems enables you to make a more conscious decision about what is best for you and to question what you have been taught to accept as truth.

Acknowledging fears of abandonment can open up a more honest dialogue with your partner and other loved ones about commitment and security. It's worth considering whether we are ever in control of anything except our responses. Irrespective of our relationships, do we ever really have control over our partners, and do we really want that?

Evangeline has recently been exploring non-monogamy with her partner, but was experiencing overthinking and anxiety when thinking about her primary partner with his secondary partner. She talked to her partner about her concerns and realized that she was just worried about losing the control she thought she had. Once she realized she wasn't losing her partner but rather a perception about the relationship, she could work through her anxiety, and her mind quieted down.

To overcome anxiety, you must recognize that it's a perfectly acceptable response to a fear of losing control. Dipping your toes into the world of non-monogamy goes against some of the deep-rooted values society has so kindly bestowed upon us. Although our worries may be running on overdrive because of this, it does not mean this lifestyle choice is out of reach. With a good support network and the acceptance that you can only change what you can control, there is no reason why you can't explore a non-monogamous relationship.

You can develop tools and coping mechanisms to help manage your feelings, such as recognizing and acknowledging your emotional responses, looking after your emotions by making time for self-care, pacing yourself in the non-monogamous world about what you can handle right now, and talking to others honestly about how you feel. From there, you can establish a better sense of control by learning to take charge of your reactions to situations and ignoring the rest. You can then channel these feelings more positively.

Demystifying Jealousy in Non-monogamy

One of the biggest hurdles many couples face when choosing non-monogamy is jealousy. It's incredible how many people find the idea of leading a polyamorous life perfectly acceptable on paper but are completely unprepared for the intensity of their emotions once it becomes a reality. Remember that part of your interest in non-monogamy is likely because you have big feelings and want to share them with more than one partner. It's normal, and it's okay!

Some folks in this realm have shared that they absolutely relish the excitement of exploring connections with multiple people. However, it's pretty amusing how their stomachs can do somersaults at the mere thought of their partner cozying up with someone else (from all the pent-up jealousy they feel). It's not because you or your partner are doing anything wrong that you're feeling jealous; it's because you haven't yet learned how to manage these feelings in this context and are still working through some old limiting beliefs.

Emily, who's bisexual, and Catherine, who's lesbian, first considered exploring non-monogamy about a year into their relationship. The monogamous relationship constrained Emily's ability to explore her sexual desires with men. Initially, Catherine was incredibly hurt and worried that this was because she wasn't enough for Emily, making her jealous. As they worked through their boundaries, rules, and insecurities, Catherine felt less jealousy - she realized it wasn't "her" problem; she couldn't physically give Emily the "equipment" she was curious about. Without discussing their emotions and concerns, Catherine would never have gained the peace of mind to escape the jealousy.

Learning to control that sneaky little green monster called jealousy is another way that non-monogamy can make you a better person.

So, what is jealousy?

In his book *Opening Up*, Tristan Taormino states that jealousy is an umbrella term for feelings, including insecurity, fear of abandonment, competitiveness, envy, possessiveness, inadequacy, feeling left out, and feeling unloved. Jealousy is a complex emotional state; saying you're jealous is vague. It manifests differently and means different things to each person. Working out why you feel "jealous" may open a Pandora's box of unresolved feelings, but you can't resolve the problems causing the emotions until you identify why. Once you know why you're jealous, you'll be better able to deal with it, feel less motivated or controlled by it, and finally let go of the feelings.[24]

One man in a non-monogamous relationship described how he felt after his partner slept with another person for the first time. He said jealousy is a dragon to be slain daily, and the only way to kill it successfully is through love and acceptance. "The first time it happens, it might be days of agony. The feeling hits you so hard that you don't know whether to vomit or cry, curl up in a ball, or sprint up a mountain."[25]

The best way for many couples to demystify jealousy is by acknowledging that it's a common emotion usually brought about by insecurity and the fear of loss.

Shifting from monogamy to non-monogamy means realizing that sometimes, your partner may want to spend time with someone else. To make this shift possible, there must be an acceptance that the person you love, who means the most to you, can be shared with others (there is that "sharing is caring" mantra again). It takes time to be accepting of your partner sharing something special with someone other than you, but it is possible with open communication, trust, and a strong foundation of love and understanding. Ultimately, embracing non-monogamy through jealousy requires prioritizing the happiness and fulfillment of all parties involved.

So how about we tackle this challenge head-on, hmm? The shift in mindset can be challenging as jealousy, fear, and insecurities arise. The good thing is that these feelings can be overcome, and your perspective can shift.

So, how do we tame that wild beast known as jealousy? It starts with recognizing the triggers and accepting the feelings rather than letting them consume you. Jealousy usually evolves from a crisis in trust, and people often experience different triggers based on personal circumstances. Analyzing and using these triggers as a means of self-awareness and working on insecurities to enhance personal growth can create a more positive outlook.

It is also worth asking yourself:

- Why are you jealous?

- What is this emotion telling you?

- Is it because you haven't set appropriate ground rules with your partner?

- Do you need to raise the level of communication with each other?

Jealousy is not unique to non-monogamy, but its complexities require more thought in this type of relationship. Some couples claim that renouncing monogamy has improved their fidelity because they can be completely honest about who they see without breaking any rules. By adding more love to each other's lives, they have increased the love within the relationship.

Once you've tackled the fear, you can embrace the freedom. Next, we'll look at the tools you can use to do precisely that.

From Fear to Freedom: Practical Tools for Overcoming Negative Emotions

Fear is a natural part of our emotional responses. Fear is our body's way of telling us we feel unsafe. It's like your internal alarm system is going off. This can stem from feeling out of control, left out, or not knowing the reaction you'll receive. Unfortunately, we can't call Ghostbusters when we're scared in real life, so we need tools to overcome the negative emotions we may experience in non-monogamous relationships.

Imagine having a toolbox for these emotions, like emotional pliers and coping wrenches. You would become a non-monogamous handyman, ready to handle anything that comes your way, emotionally speaking. Let's dive into building this toolbox and stocking it with all the emotional tools you need for an ease-filled and graceful journey ahead.

Emotional Resilience: Developing Your Handy Dandy Non-Monogamous Toolkit

Our emotional responses are like the dashboard of a car – they tell us what's going on inside and are important indicators of our mental health and personal well-being.

The first tool in your toolbox should be acceptance. Accepting that the dashboard of your car has some warning lights on. It's never a good idea to suppress your emotions or ignore how you're feeling, just like it's not a good idea to ignore the engine light and hope it doesn't explode. You may be able to conceal your feelings for a short time, but this is only a temporary solution to a much bigger problem.

Accepting your emotions can be tricky, mainly because society so kindly teaches us to be emotionless robots. However, emotions aren't bad; they're just trying to get our attention and can teach us about our needs and desires. To illustrate, you may feel anxious or upset about your partner's date; the "Check Engine" light starts blinking, telling you there is something to pay attention to here. You might be particularly concerned about that person or crave more communication and reassurance from your partner about their other relationships. Acknowledging these emotions lets you know how you're feeling and what you need from your partner to feel safe and comfortable in the relationship.

Another great tool is learning to build your emotional resilience when choosing a non-monogamous lifestyle. Developing a customized toolkit of coping strategies for when the going gets tough is paramount when managing fears, jealousy, and anxiety. There is no shame in acknowledging the validity of your emotions, but you can learn from them rather than allowing them to overwhelm you.

Naturally anxious people may find practicing self-care, mindfulness, and cognitive behavioral techniques helpful.

Here are some self-care priorities:

- **Exercise**, even in short bursts. Physical activity has been scientifically proven to reduce stress and anxiety.[26]

- **Eat a balanced diet**, stay hydrated, and regulate meal times to improve energy levels and focus.

- **Prioritize sleep** and avoid screen time for an hour or two before bed. Use blue-light-blocking glasses to avoid feeling alert when the sun goes down.

- **Contact friends and family** if you feel overwhelmed and need to talk to someone other than your partner(s), who may provide a more neutral perspective.

Below are a few mindfulness suggestions:

- **Practice gratitude and positivity** to remind yourself that these feelings are temporary, like the passing of stormy weather, and focus on *what* you are grateful for and *why*.

- **Meditation, relaxation, and breathing exercises** can be excellent ways to alleviate tension and focus on the present. Explore classes or apps, and schedule time to allow yourself to breathe and relax. If this is not for you, consider other options, such as yoga classes, which often incorporate a relaxation session.

- **Practice emotional regulation**, self-soothing techniques, and kindness. Fill your time with activities you enjoy, such as gardening, hiking, swimming, and other grounding techniques, to live in the now.

- **Practice positive self-talk**, place your hand on your heart when experiencing difficult emotions, and say, "I am kind to myself in this moment. I give myself the compassion I need." Remind yourself that jealousy is a normal reaction to figuring out how to deal with non-monogamy rather than something to be ashamed of.

Some essential cognitive behavioral techniques:

- **Practice self-awareness exercises** to manage anxiety. Develop an understanding that the inner critic is not *you* and that *you* are only the observer of your thoughts rather than the ideas themselves.

- **Challenge negative thoughts and reframe fears** to alter your perceived response to anxiety. Change the narrative and replace negative thoughts with positive and rational affirmations. Call in your inner author and re-write the story.

- **Recognize that the unlearning process takes time** by accepting the difference between the journey and destination. Allow yourself growth and enjoyment along the way.

- **Try Byron Katie's 4 Question Technique from 'The Work'** to see if your suffering stems from believing your thoughts, irrespective of whether or not they are true. The four questions to ask yourself are:

  - Is it true?

- Can you absolutely know it's true?

- How do you react/what happens when you believe that thought?

- Who would you be without the thought?

Once you've answered these questions, turn your thoughts around. This allows you to consider the opposite of what you currently believe. Consider the turnaround and see if you can find the actual parts of your life.[27]

Another excellent all-in-one self-care and mindfulness tool is journaling. Journaling your thoughts can also provide a safe space to understand and express your emotions without publicizing private feelings you are not yet ready to share with others.

The Catalyst Integration Journal Practice

The Catalyst Integration Journal Practice by Aaron Abke[28], a teacher of the Law of One and A Course In Miracles, advocates a process that allows you to question the catalyst for your feelings by following a four-step process in which you write down your answers to the following:

1. Catalyst Review: Think about a challenging experience you had, particularly one that triggered sadness, anger, or fear.

2. What emotions did you feel during this catalyst? List the order in which you felt them.

3. Write the belief linked with your emotion (e.g ., sadness—lack; anger—attachment; fear—control).

4. Ask yourself these two questions: What is this experience asking me to accept and forgive about myself? What is this experience asking me to be aware of within myself?

The above process allows you to build self-awareness so the catalyst can be used constructively. You can understand your needs and desires by exploring emotions and their underlying meanings. This method is like an emotional Swiss Army knife, allowing you to harness the catalyst as a tool for personal growth and transformation rather than allowing it to control or overwhelm you. Additionally, this process promotes self-compassion and forgiveness, as you recognize that your emotions are valid and serve as valuable sources of information about yourself.

The Five Senses Grounding Technique

You can also reduce anxiety by practicing the five senses (or 5-4-3-2-1) grounding technique, which can be used alongside breathing exercises to relieve you. This test is handy for those who find their anxiety uncontrollable or overwhelming. It's designed to change negative or panicky thought processes and reestablish current events.[29]

This technique involves focusing on the following:

- Five things you can **see**. Maybe it's your weird neighbor's garden gnome or the stain on your carpet from last year's accidental spaghetti incident.

- Four things you can **feel**. Whether it's your cat, your clothes, or your chair.

- Three things you can **hear**. It could be the distant hum of traffic, your neighbor's dog barking at everyone who walks by, or even the sweet sound of silence (if you're lucky).

- Two things you can **smell**. Be it your morning coffee or the not-so-pleasant odor of your armpits.

- One thing you can **taste**. Anything but your boogers, please. Even tasting the top of your mouth or passing your tongue around your teeth counts, but delicious food is a total plus.

Remember, this isn't a quick fix for your problems. Unlearning takes consistent practice and patience, but mindfulness can help you be more present instead of worrying about the past or the future.

Start with short meditation sessions daily and gradually increase the duration as the process becomes more natural. Remember to be kind to yourself along the way and celebrate small victories. Rome was not built in a day.

Releasing Trauma From The Body

Your body's a master at playing the panic card, thanks to good ol' adrenaline. You may be holding onto stress, tension, anxiety, or trauma without you consciously being aware of it. Your body supports you as best as possible by processing the hormones needed to heal you from stress and trauma in the way it knows how. It stores the stress in different parts of your body until you are ready to release it (if you ever are).

Here is where the plot thickens: your mind and body often play the classic good cop–bad cop routine. You may experience a green light in your mind that indicates that you are ready to do something, but your body slams on the brakes as past stored pain catches up with you.

For instance, your mind may know and accept that your partner isn't abandoning you for another person after you have both decided to adopt a non-monogamous lifestyle. You've chosen non-monogamy because you agreed that love is abundant and more love can only be good. You may even find it easier to be with another partner. Then your body pulls up the handbrake, and the thought of your partner being intimate with someone else makes you feel uncomfortable, scared, or ill.

Why, you ask? Adrenaline! This fearful yet strong troublemaker can work for or against us, and there is a fine line between the excitement of a new relationship and the fear it can generate if you aren't thrilled with the boundaries you have set as a couple. It gets worse (sorry). Your body doesn't know the difference between good adrenaline and bad adrenaline. It's like your body's emotional control center is stuck in shuffle mode, randomly switching between fight, flight, freeze, and fawn responses.

When do these responses kick in?

Fight: When you feel terrified or angry.

Flight: When you feel anxious and overthink things.

Freeze: When you dissociate or shut down.

Fawn: When you feel overwhelmed and exhibit codependent behavior.

These responses can leave you feeling upset, like your hands are tied (and not in a good way) if you don't deal with them.[30] But don't worry; there are ways to regulate your nervous system, even in the midst of them.

In his groundbreaking book, *The Body Keeps The Score*, Dr. Bessel van der Kolk explores the impact of trauma on the brain, body, and psyche and defines it as a whole-body experience. The science behind this theory considers the autonomic nervous system's reaction and the idea that if trauma disrupts the body's natural regulation systems, it cannot manage them. If we don't deal with trauma, it's stored in the body and can affect breathing, heart rate, and digestion.[31]

How do you know when your body and nervous system are dysregulated? Luckily, our bodies are brilliant, and our nervous system gives us signs and symptoms to tell us something is wrong. If you experience any of these symptoms frequently, it's time for you to give your body a reset. Look out for:

- Codependent behavior

- Feeling anxious, fearful, or angry

- Overthinking

- Feeling exhausted or overwhelmed

- Unexplained mood swings

- Depression

- Having trouble focusing or concentrating

- Dissociating or shutting down

- Being forgetful

In addition to these mental symptoms, you may experience some physical signs, including:

- Irritable bowel

- Stomach pain

- Nausea

- Shortness of breath

- Fatigue

- Irregular heartbeat or breathing

- Sweaty palms

- Weaker immune system

- Hormone dysfunction

In most cases of dysregulation, basic tasks like eating or sleeping become a challenge.[32]

A holistic approach, incorporating mental and physical processes, can be beneficial when attempting to align the mind and body. Mindfulness, meditation, and conscious breathing practices are your trust sidekicks in dealing with an overstimulated nervous system, and there are many techniques you can try to regulate these feelings - some will be more effective than others, depending on how these issues affect you.

Pro tip: Make it a habit to check in with your body throughout the day and name your emotions. Then notice any tension or other physical sensations that you need to address. Naming it creates awareness (you know, that first step we mentioned to tackling all these icky emotions).

If you notice your body is shaking, having a panic attack, or freezing up on you then here are a few different strategies to regulate your nervous system:

Shake It Out

Shaking and vibrating (which we call wiggling and jiggling your body) is known to counterbalance the nervous system and bring it back to a calm state.[33] So channel your inner Shakira and let those hips (and everything else) don't lie!

Dr. David Berceli, as part of his Tension and Trauma Release Exercises, or TRE, created neurogenic tremors (also called therapeutic tremors). Did you know these tremors can help you shake off some deep-rooted trauma? It's like giving your body a little earthquake to release all that built-up stress and tension. These neurogenic tremors regulate the nervous system by calming the parts of our brains that control emotions and stress responses. It's suggested to start at the lower parts of the body and then slowly move up the spine to the head.[34] So get ready to shake, wiggle, and jiggle your way to relaxation!

Somatic Therapy Experiences

Peter Levine created Somatic Experiencing, which dynamically revolutionized trauma treatment by putting less emphasis on the mind and more attention on the body. He worked with several ethologists as they studied animal behavior and found that animals reset their nervous systems once they've experienced a fight or flight situation.

This reset process is automatic, and they do it by using specific body movements to release excess pent-up sympathetic nervous system energy. Using these studies, Levine developed techniques humans can use to reset their nervous systems.

Although Somatic Experiencing is a trauma therapy, it focuses on nervous system regulation and is ideal for all of us to do in times of stress or anxiety. Our bodies are made to heal from trauma and stress. We just need to know how to do it.[35]

Let's take a look at each of these techniques so you can learn how to do them:

Checking Physical Comfort

Bring your attention to your physical comfort level and tune out your circumstances (this becomes easier with practice). Find a comfy chair, feet flat on the floor, and soak in the cozy goodness. Adjust until comfortable. Take a few deep breaths as you take in the calming elements around you, such as soothing colors, quirky artwork, or your trusted plushie sidekick. Spend a minute or two on this exercise until you feel like the king or queen of relaxation. How do you feel now?

Self-Soothing with Touch

Physical touch isn't just for romantic moments; it's your secret weapon for staying grounded by making yourself feel safely contained in your body. You or other people can apply this physical touch for self-soothing purposes.

Here's how to do it to yourself:

Sit and place your right hand under the left armpit and your left hand on the right shoulder. Feel your body's sensations under your hands, become aware of your heartbeat, and notice if your skin is warm or cool. Do you feel contained? Savor the experience for at least 30 seconds as you ground yourself back into your body and remind yourself you are safe.

Recalling Kindness

This technique allows your physiology to relax and settle by going down memory lane and recalling a moment of kindness and safety. Recall details of a heartwarming experience, focusing on kindness. Notice how emotions bloom, how your body reacts to the memory, and watch yourself transform as you recall the memory. How does your body feel now compared to before?

Finding Your True Self

This exercise helps you find your nervous system and emotional regulation while helping you feel grounded.

Here is how to do it:

Recall moments when you felt the most like yourself. Close your eyes and dive into those memories with as much detail as possible, almost like it's happening again with all five senses activated. Don't hold back. Explore the details and how your body responds to reliving the good old days. Consider your current feelings - do you feel different from when you started?

Calming with "Voo" Sound

This one sounds a little kooky (and you'll definitely look and sound a bit kooky doing it). Still, the Voo sound technique is a powerful way to settle your nervous system and make you feel a sense of calm and ease, especially in your body's core, as the vibrations move through your torso and organs. Trust us, it's worth looking and sounding a bit wacky for this one. This is a solo performance, so pick your stage – maybe your car, garden, or a bathroom where no one can judge your newfound vocal talents.

Here are the steps:

Create a low "Voo" sound like a foghorn. Breathe deeply and feel the vibrations in your body as it goes down your vocal cords to your pelvic floor. As your breath gently runs out, allow the next breath to come in slowly and naturally. If calming, repeat up to 2-3 times. How do you feel now?

Deep Breathing

Deep breathing is a surprisingly simple yet effective method of calming the nerves.[36] The best part is that it can be done anywhere at any time, which makes it a great tool to keep in your back pocket. When we slow our breathing by taking deep, intentional breaths (especially out-breaths), we tell our parasympathetic nervous system to calm down. This restores our mental and emotional state and releases anxiety and stress.

Spending a few minutes daily doing breathwork can revolutionize your mental health and help your nervous system better process stress and anxiety. It can also help you level up as a Zen Master (who doesn't want ultimate inner peace?). You can use apps (we love Calm and Head-space) or practice yoga breathing (pranayama). Pranayama combines breathing with yoga (two birds, one stone) and allows you to achieve a state of calm.[37]

Drink A Cup of Tea

As crazy as it sounds, certain teas can impact your central nervous system. These teas are made with specific herbs, called nervines, that relax your nervous system, ease tension and anxiety, and reduce chronic stress.[38] You can match the herbs to your needs:

- Chamomile (acute stress)

- Holy Basil (stress and depression)

- Milky Oat (nervous exhaustion)

- Skullcap (muscular stress and tension)

- Passionflower (anxiety and desperation)

Become A Glimmer Seeker

Deb Dana, a licensed clinical trauma social worker, coined the term "glimmers." In her book, *The Polyvagal Theory of Therapy,* she uses the word "glimmers" to refer to the tiny moments in perfect synergy—regulated and connected with the world around us.[39] In other words, it's your ticket to calming the nervous system and finding your happy place. Each glimmer that you notice around you tells your nervous system that all is well.

Glimmers are the opposite of triggers and help calm the nervous system by finding the beauty of each moment. They are all around you, all the time; all you have to do is practice being a glimmer detective whenever you feel called to. With time, this practice becomes your secret superpower, healing you more and more with each glimmer you find.

Self-Care and Independence as a Priority: Taking Care of Your Mental Health

Independence and interdependence are essential aspects of any relationship, including non-monogamous ones. Just as nature beautifully balances these principles, relationships can thrive when they incorporate both elements harmoniously.

In nature, we see how individual species and organisms maintain their independence. Each flower, tree, and creature possesses its own unique traits and functions, contributing to the ecosystem's diversity. Similarly, in relationships, whether monogamous or non-monogamous, individual partners retain their identities, interests, and personal growth. Accepting independence means recognizing and valuing each person's need for self-discovery, personal goals, and time alone.

Self-care is like a tree tending to its roots. Like plants, people in relationships need self-care to stay mentally healthy. Recognizing the importance of self-care lets each partner recharge and grow individually, which is good for the general health of the relationship. Like a well-fed and watered plant, self-care helps people be their best in life and relationships.

Treat your self-care as a priority and carve out time to practice it regularly to cultivate positive habits to release trauma from the body and mind. With the correct time and investment in yourself, you'll slowly but surely instill a sense of calm and emotional well-being.

Self-care is not selfish. It is instrumental in maintaining a healthy mind and body, particularly when navigating non-monogamous relationships. It would help if you never neglected your well-being for the sake of a relationship. If you find yourself in a situation where you are not allowed space for yourself, you need to make the time and space to carve it out of your day, even if that means losing some time with your partner(s). Please think of the scenario in an airplane: first, put on your air mask before helping others with theirs. The same goes for relationships - you won't be able to fully support, nourish, and love your partner(s) if you don't do the same for yourself. A better you for you is a better you for them too.

Think about creating and developing your own personalized self-care toolbox next to your non-monogamous toolbox. Which techniques would be most beneficial for your mental health? Do you find happiness in engaging with others in dancing or yoga classes? Or would a more private pastime such as journaling, Reiki, or meditation prove more effective? Can you think of alternative activities that would bring you out of anxiety and worry, enabling you to relax and develop a more positive mindset? Investigate these to learn more about yourself and what is best for you.

Support Systems and Interdependence: Leveraging Resources for Mental Health

Nature also reveals how connection promotes harmony. Bees pollinate flowers, trees shelter animals, and ecosystems thrive on symbiotic relationships. In non-monogamous relationships, interdependence takes on a beautiful form. Partners recognize that while they are distinct entities, their lives weave together in a tapestry of shared experiences, emotions, and growth. Just as a forest thrives when its members collaborate, non-monogamous relationships can flourish when partners communicate openly, support one another, and cultivate a sense of togetherness.

Similar to how diverse ecosystems depend on each other, relationships benefit from partners leaning on each other for support. Recognizing the importance of interdependence in non-monogamous relationships includes being attuned to each other's mental health. Partners can offer emotional support, understanding, and encouragement as they navigate life's challenges together. Just as various species in nature rely on one another, interdependence in relationships strengthens the bond between partners.

As we have already established, a robust support system is necessary to ensure mental well-being in non-monogamous relationships. However, this is about more than maintaining strong communication with your partner(s). You may need backup from friends and family, too.

Be bold and lean on your support network—the other pieces of your ecosystem outside of your partners—for help during times of difficulty or uncertainty. They can offer an alternative perspective without sharing the heightened emotions you may be feeling.

However, if you feel like you're lacking support from the people around you or that your non-monogamous lifestyle is misunderstood, there are other places you can turn to seek help and advice:

- Talk to people who have navigated similar anxieties and experiences.

- Check out online groups such as Facebook's Polyamory Support Group, Reddit's r/polyamory and r/nonmonogamy communities, or the *Non-Monogamy Help* podcast to find resources, help, and others navigating similar journeys.

- Seek professional resources such as therapists specializing in non-monogamy who can offer targeted advice and coping strategies.

- Look at online resources, like the National Coalition for Sexual Freedom's Kink And Poly Aware Professionals Directory (KAP), to find non-monogamy-friendly professionals.

- Online platforms like Talkspace or BetterHelp can also connect you with licensed therapists from the comfort of your home.

Balancing Independence and Interdependence

The dance between independence and interdependence is a delicate one. Just as a river can flow independently while contributing to the vast ocean, partners can nurture their individuality while embracing the connection they share with others. It is beneficial for partners in non-monogamous relationships to discuss their needs, wants, and the agreements and boundaries that shape the connection and support each person in opening up together.

Prioritizing mental health through self-care makes this delicate dance even better. When individuals take steps to maintain their emotional well-being, they're better equipped to communicate effectively, set boundaries, and engage in relationships with authenticity. Much like a river's flow is influenced by its source, each partner's ability to communicate and relate is enriched when rooted in a foundation of self-care.

Nature's elegance can teach us to appreciate each partner's uniqueness and contribution to the relationship's ecology. While cherishing our lifelong relationships, we can realize that a network's strength comes from its interwoven strands. Independent, interdependent, and self-care in non-monogamous partnerships (and most other relationships) can lead to a rewarding and joyful journey for all involved, just like nature's delicate balance maintains life.

Remember, the whole world is a part of your interconnected forest - how you water and nourish each tree is up to you. Now that we've looked at dealing with negative emotions and mental well-being, we'll look at the importance of communication in non-monogamous relationships.

The Secret Sauce of Non-monogamous Conversation

∞

Just like a well-prepared kitchen sets the stage for a delightful meal, communication is the essential ingredient for a thriving relationship. But without the right seasonings, you'll end up with a bland dish, and that's where transparency becomes your secret sauce. We communicate with our significant others daily, but there is a Grand Canyon-sized difference between the "What's for dinner?" chats and opening up about your feelings, especially when your relationships involve more than one partner.

Now, think of communication styles as different cooking methods in the grand kitchen of relationships. Some are skilled with chef knives, subtle yet assertive. Others are fiery grillmasters, bold and direct. Others savor the slow simmer, the passive communications. No matter your preferred culinary approach, using a combination of tools in your communication style allows for precise, transparent, and deep conversations where your true feelings and emotions are made clear, and a delicious relationship masterpiece can be created.

Non-monogamous relationships are like a daring culinary project. They require those tough conversations about insecurity, trust issues, and flavors of jealousy. Just like a chef chooses ingredients carefully, you'll need to establish boundaries and rules to ensure everyone in the relationship savors the same recipe. Once those boundaries are set, you can unleash your creativity and season your relationship with the most vibrant and exotic flavors.

In this section, we will learn the importance of open and honest communication and gain practical tips to turn your relationship into a culinary masterpiece worthy of a Michelin-starred restaurant.

Transparency and Honesty in the Recipe of Love

Picture non-monogamy as running a bustling gourmet restaurant with a group of talented chefs. Like in the kitchen, trust, honesty, and transparency are essential. The meals may differ every time without honesty about each ingredient and transparency for each measurement.

Like running a fine-dining establishment, non-monogamy can be a rewarding and fulfilling lifestyle choice, requiring diligent effort. Keeping the lines of communication open among your culinary team is essential, regularly checking in to ensure everyone is on the same page, preventing any unexpected flavors (or emotions) from ruining the exquisite dining experience. So, whether you're crafting gourmet dishes or navigating non-monogamous relationships, remember, it's all about the perfect recipe of trust, honesty, and transparency.

Now, let's delve into crafting your non-monogamous love recipe. Just like in the kitchen, where precise measurements and harmonious flavors are key, consider careful communication and an unwavering focus on your partners' ever-evolving desires, needs, and emotions.

In this culinary journey of relationships, you're the master chef, continually refining your unique concoction. Yet, akin to adding spices thoughtfully, there's a distinction between honesty and complete transparency. We often yearn to hide certain secret ingredients like judgment or resentment, dreading criticism or backlash. But for the symphony of non-monogamous love to flourish, you must embrace the courage to unveil your innermost thoughts and perceived imperfections.

Just as every spice contributes to a dish's depth, your quirks, and vulnerabilities add to the richness of your relationships. So ask yourself: "What flavors am I hesitant to share?" Remember, the medley of ingredients creates a genuinely delicious masterpiece in both the kitchen and your love life.

People hide details like PINs, passwords, text messages, social media accounts, and email accounts. We are inherently programmed (primarily by society) to maintain our privacy, avoid confrontation, and downplay our mistakes - Big Brother's watching, right?

Now, while some secrets are as precious as grandma's secret cookie recipe, others can turn our relationships into a recipe for disaster. The healthiest relationship is one with no secrecy, in which all participants feel they can be sincere without judgment or criticism. Unless, of course, you're secretly Batman, and revealing your true identity could jeopardize Gotham's safety.

Non-monogamy is a journey of self-discovery, and being upfront about feelings, needs, and desires is even more critical when more people are involved. It requires a specific personality shift for some people to be able to express their deepest fantasies and desires. Still, being the most authentic version of yourself can be gratifying and liberating, like going from mild-mannered Clark Kent to cape-wearing Superman.

It is equally important to voice negative thoughts before they become harmful or all-consuming, in addition to being honest about positive feelings. Failure to share your anxieties and concerns if you are jealous of one of your lover's partners will result in resentment and, eventually, break the relationship.

Imagine a monogamous couple where one partner secretly starts seeing someone else. When the truth finally emerges, it can cause pain and be potentially relationship-ending. Honesty, much like a well-seasoned dish, is always the best policy.

Talking openly about feelings and working through problems before they become an issue is healthier for everyone. It may be the difference between saving a relationship or ensuring an amicable separation - no one wants to be blindsided, and being in a non-monogamous relationship can allow for open, honest communication.

Tools of the Trade: Communication Recipes

Cooking up meaningful conversations in your non-monogamous relationship is like making a perfect soufflé – it takes time, patience, and the right ingredients.

For timing, discussing your deepest feelings when you're both rushing off to work is like trying to bake a cake in a microwave – it's just not gonna work! Just as patience is the yeast that helps bread rise to perfection, giving each person time to speak their minds in your conversation ensures it doesn't turn out as flat as a pancake.

Now, let's examine some of the juiciest techniques for actively engaging with your partner with the right ingredients:

Active, Compassionate Listening involves entirely focusing on the person speaking by giving them your entire presence, not interrupting them, and responding thoughtfully. It is a powerful tool in any relationship, especially non-monogamous ones, and encourages you to savor every word, feeling, and thought without adding any judgment to the mix.[40] An excellent demonstration of an appropriate response to this is if your partner is expressing jealousy. Instead of dismissing their feelings, you could say, "I hear you're jealous. That sounds tough. Let's talk about what we can do to address this."

"I" Statements are a good way for partners to express feelings and needs without blaming or criticizing.[41] If a partner wants to express their feelings, they could say, "I feel anxious when you spend the night at Bob's place and don't text me goodnight," rather than, "You make me anxious when you don't text me from Bob's."

Nonviolent Communication Breakdown (NVC) is a means of expressing yourself with empathy and understanding, which involves stating feelings, needs, observations, and requests without blaming, criticizing, or judging your partner(s).[42]

The NVC technique could be used in non-monogamous relationships in the following ways when jealousy stirs the pot of a partner's new connection:

- **Observation**: "I noticed you've been spending more time with your new partner lately."

- **Feeling**: "I feel anxious and insecure about your connection with them."

- **Need**: "I need reassurance and open communication to help me process these feelings."

- **Request**: "Could we have a calm and honest conversation about how I'm feeling and find ways to support each other during this change?"

By sprinkling these techniques into your conversations, you'll create a delightful space for discussing emotions, navigating the complexities of non-monogamous relationships, and fostering understanding, empathy, and support. This approach will let your connection simmer to perfection in your non-monogamous journey, just like a sumptuous stew on the stove.

Food for Thought: Deciphering Non-Verbal Signals

Spending enough time with your partner gives you the superpower to decode non-verbal signals and respond appropriately to those cues. It may be more intuitive than conscious, but we constantly send messages to others through body language, mannerisms, and facial expressions before we utter a word. Non-verbal communication can be as expressive as the hand gestures of the Italians or as subtle as a sly, raised eyebrow during a secret conversation.

Our posture, eye contact, and activity level often reveal our true feelings before we even say a word. Our body language tells people if we are happy, sad, angry, or nervous. Awareness of our body language and understanding how it can impact our interactions with others is essential for effective communication. By paying attention to our nonverbal cues, we can better express ourselves and ensure that our intentions are accurately conveyed, fostering stronger connections and understanding in our relationships.

Consider how you respond physically to a friend versus your behavior in a job interview. You will likely adopt a neutral expression and an unconsciously upright and confident posture for a job interview. You will be less nervous and more relaxed around a friend or partner. You may even let out a fart or two around them, but you would never dare do that around a hiring manager. The situations and people involved inform your behavior, verbally and non-verbally.

Let's feast on some delectable tidbits about non-verbal communication:

- Non-verbal communication plays a crucial role in expressing feelings and emotions.[43] You can enhance your understanding and empathy by being aware of non-verbal cues. To become a better communicator, it is just as vital that you acknowledge the signals you are sending as it is to be sensitive to what the body language of others is telling us.

- Pay close attention to body language, facial expressions, and tone of voice. These can provide valuable insights into your partner's feelings and emotions.

- Be aware of your own non-verbal cues. Make sure your body language and tone of voice match your words. They should go together like peanut butter and jelly. If we say one thing and our bodies say another, we will likely come across as dishonest, incongruent, or inauthentic. If our non-verbal cues match our verbal ones, we can establish trust and rapport better.

- Our non-verbal actions are the garnish that shows how much we genuinely care and whether or not we are listening or telling the truth.

- Remember that silence can also be a form of communication. Giving your partner space to think, process, and enjoy a cup of wine to calm down can often be more effective than words.

In his book, *The Importance of Effective Communication*, Dr. Edward Wertheim explains the five roles of non-verbal communication as follows:[44]

- **Repetition**: Like adding a pinch of salt to any dish, repetition often strengthens the message you're making verbally. Say what you mean, say it clearly, and say it often.

- **Contradiction**: Would you ever serve spaghetti ice cream at a party? No. It would confuse the masses and be unsatisfying. Then why would you say yes while shaking your head no? Contradictions convey the point you are making confusingly, thus indicating to your listener that you may not be telling the truth (consciously or unconsciously). Don't say one thing if your body is telling you another story!

- **Substitution**: An action as a substitute for a verbal message. Your facial expression often conveys a far more vivid message than words ever can. Speaking with your facial expressions, eyes, hands, and body language can say more than what comes out of your mouth.

- **Complementing**: It may add to or complement your verbal message (like fresh basil on a pizza). As a partner, if you rub your partner's back in addition to giving praise, it can increase the impact of your message while creating a tender bond.

- **Accenting**: This may accentuate or underline a verbal message. Pounding the table, for example, can highlight the importance of your message or represent your mood.

Navigating Rough Seas: Difficult Conversations

You will inevitably face difficult conversations in non-monogamous relationships but can develop strategies to navigate them with due care and respect. You need to know the steps you can take when jealousy and insecurity worm their way into your psyche and negative emotions take you by surprise. There is no "prize" in this kind of surprise.

In non-monogamous relationships, you'll need to adjust to knowing your partner is seeing other people. This may bring up fears and insecurities long laid beneath the surface. What if your partner develops feelings for another person? What if they like them more? This is all completely normal! But knowing this and dealing with it are two different things altogether. So, how might you manage your emotions in this situation?

We will look at a step-by-step process that may help you navigate the stormy seas of self-doubt, mistrust, and uncertainty during non-monogamy.

Step 1: Pause and Self-Reflect

Take time to reflect on your emotions and thoughts about the conflict. Understand your perspective and feelings before engaging in conversation. This gives you some time to calm down and enables you to recognize whether or not your thoughts are valid before going into a discussion with all guns blazing.

Step 2: Check In

All agreements, boundaries, and rules must be adhered to. Before jumping to conclusions, assessing whether any of these have been inadvertently breached is a good idea. If you doubt a partner's intentions, clarify your assumptions and talk to them calmly. Approach the situation with curiosity rather than negativity, and seek to understand and find verification rather than assume.

Step 3: Choose the Right Time and Place

Carve out time and privacy for an emotionally safe conversation. A conversation about feelings is best served in a private, emotionally safe environment, not in the middle of a crowded restaurant. Conversations in public rather than private locations are less likely to be beneficial, as your partner may zone out and focus on the inappropriateness of the place rather than the topic.

Step 4: Practice Compassionate Communication

Start the conversation gently. Assess your emotional stability before approaching the discussion, and go into the conversation with an open heart. Allow yourself to be emotionally transparent and honest with yourself. Be aware of your partner's emotions going into the conversation (they may be on high alert) and remind each other why you are here having this conversation in the first place - because you love each other (aww).

Practice the principles of nonviolent communication to express yourself with understanding and empathy. Employ "I" statements to share observations, feelings, needs, and requests. Ensure you acknowledge and validate one another's feelings throughout the conversation. Dismissing or minimizing a partner's insecurities is not conducive to happiness. Acknowledge the emotion and work through it with each other to find a solution that works for you both.

Step 5: Active, Compassionate Listening

Practice active listening by allowing each person to express their thoughts and emotions without interruption.

Be present and attentive when it's your turn to listen, and allow your partner to feel heard using reflective listening techniques. For instance, "I understand that when I talk to him, I come across as dismissive to you. I acknowledge that this makes you feel disconnected."

Step 6: Focus on Goals (Common and Solo)

Remember what made you decide to take this path at the outset? Identify the values and goals that unite your relationship. Use these shared objectives to overcome conflicts and perceived power imbalances where one person feels the other has more power in the relationship.

Remember when we mentioned writing down your *reason* for choosing non-monogamy? This is an excellent time to pull that statement out and remind yourself of why you decided to make the choice of non-monogamy. This will allow you to realign with your anchor to focus on the values and goals of your relationship(s).

Step 7: Avoid Escalation

Try to remain calm and respectful in your approach and avoid hurtful language or personal attacks. Yelling at one another drowns out the messages you are trying to impart and distracts you from the original problem. Avoid emotional dysregulation by setting boundaries for acceptable behavior before problems arise and avoiding disparaging remarks in the heat of the moment.

Step 8: Take a Break if Needed

If emotions become overwhelming and escalate into an argument or fight, have the good sense to take a break and resume the conversation later rather than shouting at one another or giving each other the silent treatment.

A study found that after taking a 20-minute break during a disagreement where the couples didn't talk (just read magazines), the participants' heart rates returned to their baselines. The conversations following the break changed dramatically. Most participants' affection and sense of humor had returned.[45]

Step 9: Seek Mediation

Some relationships may benefit from the help of a neutral mediator within the relationship or from employing a therapist to facilitate a constructive conversation. A neutral party can often help both parties find an impartial resolution by bringing a less emotional viewpoint to the discussion. Think of it as calling in a seasoned chef to taste-test your creation. A neutral party can add a pinch of objectivity to the mix.

Step 10: Focus on Solutions

Once you have gotten to the bottom of whatever problem you are experiencing, it is worthwhile to collaboratively brainstorm solutions, considering shared interests and goals, to resolve situations. When seeking answers, make sure you are open to compromise to help you reach a mutual agreement.

Step 11: Forgive and Let Go

Practice forgiveness (call in that inner Zen master again) and release any tension or lingering resentment toward your partner. Let go of that lingering resentment like you're dropping a heavy bag of emotional bricks. It's tough but worth it.

This can be easier said than done, but working towards a solution together may help you value each other as problem-solvers instead of adversaries. This, in turn, may help reignite your desire for one another, present growth opportunities, and create a stronger bond between you and your partner(s).

With forgiveness, conflict resolution is more likely. Scientists studying forgiveness found that forgiveness is one of the most significant factors in a healthy relationship. Studies also showed that couples who forgive each other are more likely to have longer, happier, and more satisfying relationships.[46]

Step 12: Celebrate Growth

Remember to celebrate small victories in your communication journey. Acknowledge each other's efforts to improve well-being and learn together. Speak to one another clearly and remind each other that regular conversations and open communication will help develop trust, prevent misunderstandings, and alleviate jealousy and anxiety. Regular check-ins help establish a safe space to express emotions and seek reassurance.

So, there you have it – the 12 steps to navigate those conflicting non-monogamous conversations. Hopefully, these communication techniques will assist you and remind you that the feelings you are experiencing are not uncommon or invalid. All emotions are messengers, and your doubts, insecurities, and worries are valid and worthy of exploration. It's essential to approach them with curiosity and compassion - for yourself and your partners.

Remember that growth and self-discovery often go hand in hand with discomfort, and embracing these emotions can lead to deeper connections and personal development. Trust in the process and be patient with yourself. Remember that non-monogamy is a unique journey that requires ongoing communication, self-reflection, and a commitment to personal growth.

In the next chapter, we will look at developing healthy, consensual boundaries and limitations in a way that feels right for you and your partner(s).

Your Review Can Help Others

"To serve one is to serve all." - The Law of One, Carla Rueckert

Are you ready to be a catalyst for change in the world of relationships? As you continue your journey through this book, you're not just embarking on a personal exploration - you're stepping into a role that can transform the lives of countless others.

Help us share this knowledge and experience with others so they can have more of what we all genuinely desire—love.

If you've found value in the pages you've read thus far, we encourage you to share your insights with those who could benefit.

Every word you write in your review is a step towards a revolution in relationships. By sharing your experiences and the wisdom you've gained, you're helping others chart their course toward the love and intimacy they desire.

Simply by expressing how this book has enriched your life and what lies within its pages, you'll help others grasp that love isn't just an emotion; it's a dynamic force that requires action and unwavering commitment.

Thank you for joining us in our mission to serve others through the power of love and understanding. Together, we illuminate the path to deeper connections and lasting joy.

Crafting Healthy Boundaries and Agreements

Implementing boundaries in a relationship allows you to assert how you would like to be treated and consider how your actions may affect others. In monogamous relationships, this is relatively straightforward, as you only have to think about the feelings of one other person. Plus, society kindly lays out all the boundaries for you before you even start (how nice of them). At the outset, there is an unspoken rule that only two people, and no more, will be in the relationship. No third-wheelers allowed! Although couples may implement further practices as their relationship evolves, this is a far more simplistic starting point.

In multi-person relationships, setting boundaries becomes a delicate dance where you must consider the feelings of not just one but many, including your own.

Like our favorite pizza toppings, relationships and our feelings and beliefs about them evolve.

Finding that sweet spot of what works for us at the beginning of a relationship could change dramatically, depending on our experiences and the people we meet. Boundaries are as unique as snowflakes and are very personal, so it is essential to recognize that what may work for one person could make another feel uncomfortable. It is not a one-size-fits-all approach.

However, consider a few rules as an absolute minimum when establishing personal boundaries. These should apply not only to consensual non-monogamous relationships but to all healthy relationships, irrespective of your physical and emotional beliefs:

- You are not a puppet, which means no one should be playing puppet master pulling your strings. Please don't allow anyone to manipulate or coerce you into doing something you aren't comfortable with, and don't go twisting anyone's arm to do things they're not into.

- Let's keep things friendly and fun! Don't tolerate yelling, name-calling, or disparaging remarks from other people, and maintain a respectful tone when talking to others. It's all about spreading good vibes and positivity!

- Self-ownership is necessary in the school of life. Don't blame other people for things that are your responsibility. Be accountable for your actions, and don't accept blame for items that are not your fault.

- Accept that, while valid, your feelings are your own, and another person may have an entirely different perspective on the exact same situation. It's like we're all wearing different-colored glasses, seeing the world in our own unique way. Practice empathy for other people's viewpoints, regardless of their differences.

- Accept that you have the right to request space and time away from a situation, enjoy your personal bubble, and that others have the same right.

These are just starting points, Boundaries 101 if you may, but they should provide a stepping stone to thinking about your needs, wants, and desires and enable you to establish rules that work for you and your partner(s) in your relationships. Respecting each other's boundaries is critical to developing and maintaining trust in non-monogamous relationships.

Understanding the Importance of Boundaries and Agreements

To understand the importance of boundaries and agreements in non-monogamous relationships, we need to be able to differentiate between them.

In their simplest form, boundaries are set by a person regarding their mental and physical needs and limits (they don't force anyone else to do something; they dictate what you are or aren't prepared to accept). It's like you have your own personal no-fly zones in the vast landscape of relationships.

Agreements are a collective activity where each person's boundaries are considered to create rules. They're like your relationship's constitution, ensuring everyone is on the same page.

Boundaries and agreements are like two peas in a pod, working hand in hand to make your relationship thrive. Boundaries are your individual shields, protecting your emotional fortress. Agreements, on the other hand, are the communal guidelines that ensure everyone respects those boundaries.

Think of it like a well-choreographed dance. Boundaries set the stage, and agreements are the dancers gracefully moving within those boundaries. It's a harmonious symphony of individual needs and collective understanding.

Let's look at boundaries and rules a bit further:

Boundaries

A boundary is a personal limit or edge put in place to protect your emotional well-being, values, and autonomy. A person sets boundaries to safeguard themselves. A boundary is an individual response based on emotional needs and comfort levels. Although we might visualize boundaries as invisible barriers, they are not intended to restrict freedoms but to promote guidelines to create a safe environment for everyone. Like property lines, boundaries represent the physical and emotional space between people and mark where one person ends and another starts.[47]

Some people might picture boundaries as rigid, suffocating walls, but that's not the case! They're more like helpful road signs on the highway of love. Think of them as the "Slow Down" signs before a dangerous emotional curve.

What's a boundary for one person might be a walk in the park for another. This highlights the importance of effective communication and the need for all parties to know what is and isn't okay for each person. Although it may sound restrictive and a little tedious, learning each other's boundaries at the outset and maintaining regular check-ins can prevent problems before they arise and keep everybody happy and feeling respected and safe. It's like trying to guess someone's pizza toppings – you're better off asking!

Chris and Kyle have been in a non-monogamous relationship for eight years. Chris is uncomfortable with having sex with Kyle unless he practices safe sex and passes an STD test each month. Chris doesn't mind what Kyle decides to do with his secondary partners, but he draws the line at feeling safe sexually. Kyle understands this boundary and ensures he always practices safe sex, including when he has oral sex and submits to the STD test happily - nothing is more important to him than respecting Chris's boundaries.

Here are a few ideas of boundaries found in non-monogamous relationships:

- **Physical Boundaries:** The physical boundaries may include regular STD testing, disclosure of possible health risks, safe sex practices, and off-limits physical behavior (like spanking or choking). An example of a physical boundary is: "You can sleep with anyone you want. I do not control you, your body, or what you do. But before you have sex with me, I need you to do an STD test, which must be clear. If it's unclear, I will not have sex with you."

- **Emotional Boundaries:** All partners establish emotional boundaries by communicating what they do and don't want to know about their partner's other relationships. Emotional boundaries may also include what type of behavior makes each person feel unsafe. An example of an emotional boundary is: "I don't want to be shouted at or spoken to aggressively, so I will leave this conversation until you calm down."

- **Privacy Boundaries:** These boundaries involve chats about whether partners are okay with other partners knowing about their private details. An example of a privacy boundary is: "I don't want your lover to know details about my family, friends, job, etc. Please keep my information private."

- **Time Boundaries:** Partners can set boundaries on their time with other partners or by themselves. An example of a time boundary is: "I need two nights per week to have a few hours alone to work on my mental health by doing things I enjoy."

Agreements

In a non-monogamous arrangement, all parties create and consent to an agreement. You will decide the rules collectively, and an agreement results from a mutual consensus on the rules that govern the relationship. Theoretically, everyone is at the ship's helm and steering in the same direction, trying not to crash into any icebergs.

Agreements are a necessary tool to support the longevity of a relationship – it's like having a GPS for relationships. They ensure that everyone is on the same page and feels happy with the arrangement, not just in that moment but also in the future. All parties in non-monogamous relationships must adhere to the relationship agreement if the arrangement is going to succeed. It provides clarity, defines expectations for all, and is an essential framework based on communication, trust, and mutual respect.

To give you an idea of an agreement: "I don't want to wait for the results of an STD test to have sex with you. So, are you open to creating an agreement that we'll practice safe sex with others and will let each other know if we sleep with anyone else before we have sex?" Another could be as simple as the primary partners dedicating one night a week to each other or the partners agreeing to put their phones away while spending time together.

Such an arrangement reassures everyone involved that they have given consent to enter into a reliable, trustworthy, emotionally safe space. It is also a helpful reference tool for addressing and navigating any conflicts and can act as a reminder if anyone is unsure of what is and isn't acceptable.

Here are a few examples of agreements found in non-monogamous relationships:

- **Communication Agreement:** The partners can agree on how much or little communication happens about their other relationships. This can be anything from weekly updates to an occasional message with an emoji. It can also involve agreements about how much each partner will communicate with their secondary partners while together.

- **Transparency Agreement:** Partners can agree to disclose all new encounters or relationships to their primary partner or all partners to ensure everyone is aware of the possible dynamic change. This can foster trust, communication, and a shared understanding of the evolving romantic landscape.

- **Social Agreement:** Agreements can be made about how partners handle social situations, like interacting with friends and family or attending events. For instance, you may agree that only primary partners will attend family gatherings, but going to a movie or music concert is okay with any partner.

- **Safe Sex Agreement:** Partners can agree about STD testing and safe sex practices to ensure the safety and health of all involved. Not to mention to avoid any unwanted surprises.

- **Prioritization Agreement:** Each partner can agree to prioritize aspects of their relationship, like having quality time or addressing issues respectfully and timely. This agreement involves partners prioritizing different aspects of their relationships to ensure fairness, harmony, and emotional well-being for everyone involved, including quality time, date nights, and resolving conflicts in a timely manner.

In a relationship without agreements, misunderstandings can result in hurt feelings. To demonstrate: jealousy and insecurities will likely surface if parties engage in activities assumed by others to infringe upon the arrangement. If the relationship lacks established ground rules, a partner may feel they can call their other partner anytime, even if that means disrupting their time with another person. This is likely going down poorly! If you don't want to end up in the doghouse, talk to each other about what is acceptable.

As with boundaries, **agreements** have different features that allow us to understand them, including:

- **Joint Decisions:** An agreement involves mutual decisions between two or more people and defines specific expectations, terms, and actions.

- **Mutual Obligations:** An agreement creates shared responsibility where all parties commit to specific actions and behaviors based on the understanding.

- **Behavioral Guidelines:** The terms of an agreement often involve specific actions or behaviors, outlining what is expected and accepted in the relationship.

- **External Regulation:** An agreement regulates external actions and behaviors within a relationship. These can include spending habits, shared activities, and communication patterns.

Relationships without agreements can result in misunderstandings about expectations, leading to unintentional breaches of trust. Without an accord, parties rely on assumptions and may engage in activities others may not be comfortable with. A lack of guidance can lead to unmet needs and feelings of disconnection or self-limiting behaviors as partners rely on guesswork. When a partner's actions or decisions contradict another person's implicit expectations, it can lead to a breakdown in trust and cause emotional turmoil. Consequently, this can lead to feelings of resentment.

However, we can turn this around by learning to set boundaries and healthily make agreements.

Steps to Setting Healthy Boundaries

Suppose you are finding it difficult to set boundaries. In that case, start by looking inward and reflecting on previous relationships. Think about situations in which you felt unhappy or felt taken for granted. These emotions often indicate areas where boundaries need to be established. Discuss these with your partner(s).

This does not mean you need to dramatize or embellish events that are not relevant to the topic at hand. However, it may help you determine which behaviors were toxic to the relationship and ask yourself what you could do to prevent this from happening.

Avoid overburdening yourself by enforcing too many rules simultaneously, especially if you're establishing boundaries in a long-term partnership. This isn't like cramming for an exam - you don't need to do it all in one night. Negative behaviors can often be habitual, and it can be tricky to change them and not revert to your "old ways." Take it slow and tackle issues as they pop up, like a superhero fighting one baddie at a time.

Boundaries are not always about intimacy or sex. To demonstrate, you could set a rule with your primary partner regarding what activities you're comfortable exploring in your secondary relationships and what is reserved for your primary partner alone. Determine which practices are most important to you and develop them over time.

Developing self-awareness and understanding your needs is vital before establishing what they should be.

If you are a chronic people-pleaser, you might find it challenging to put yourself first, but you are just as important as everyone else in this arrangement, and your needs matter, too. You might find it helpful to ask yourself the following questions before making any decisions:

- What boundaries can I set to prioritize my mental, emotional, and physical well-being? How can I ensure self-care?

- What do I value most in my relationships, and how can I confirm those values are upheld in a non-monogamous context?

- What emotional connections are acceptable to

me outside of our relationship?

- Are there specific boundaries related to sexual health practices that I feel are important to establish?

- How much information do I want about my partner's other relationships? What kind of disclosure feels right for me?

- Are there any activities or behaviors I feel uncomfortable with us engaging in with other partners?

- How much time do I need for myself and each partner? How can I ensure that I balance my time effectively?

- What boundaries do I need to maintain my sense of security and emotional well-being?

- Do I have any past experiences or triggers I should be mindful of in my non-monogamous journey?

Remember that you should be open to the fact that your answers may change over time. You should answer them from your current perspective and revisit your responses regularly to ensure your ideals haven't changed. Be open to the fact that things will change, and enjoy the journey!

Once you have determined your boundaries, communicate them clearly and assertively with your partner(s). There is no need to be a boundary dictator. Still, everyone must understand and respect your feelings, so make sure you express yourself clearly without allowing statements to be vague or half-hearted. To illustrate: "I need freedom" is ambiguous and less helpful than "I need to be able to at least talk to whoever I want." Give actionable and straightforward specifics: *What* do you want, and *who/when/how/where* do you want it?

Respecting boundaries is like following traffic rules – even if you think red lights are boring, you gotta stop. If your partner wants to keep some relationship details in the vault, don't go all secret agent on them. But if it's eating at you, talk it out. Say something like, "I get that this topic bugs you, but not knowing anything makes me a nervous wreck. How can we fix this?"

And remember, it's not just about your rules; it's also about respecting the boundaries set by your partner's other lovers (metamours). Harmony is the name of the game, so play nice with everyone involved.

Finally, ask if you're scratching your head over anyone's boundaries. Although these conversations can be challenging to begin with, clarity is fundamental. Let's say that what one person defines as sex could refer only to intercourse, but for others, it could encompass all aspects of intimacy, from kissing and beyond.

Remember to celebrate the successful implementation and respect limitations in your relationship, like your favorite team won the Super Bowl. All relationships require effort, but maintaining a healthy, non-monogamous dynamic is particularly challenging, and all parties' commitment should not go unrewarded.

Creating Healthy Relationship Agreements

We have acknowledged that partners should be mindful that relationship agreements are not set in stone and that all parties should be able to communicate any changes if and when they arise.

To encourage you and your partner to communicate needs, desires, and comfort levels openly, it is a good idea to ask yourself some questions (don't worry, it's not a quiz) when alone and then meet to discuss your individual responses. Actively listening to each other's perspectives and being willing to negotiate and adapt to each other's needs while co-creating relationship agreements helps to build a foundation of mutual trust and understanding in the partnership.

The following questions are ideas of topics you and your partner may feel the need to discuss to create a successful relationship agreement:

- How do I picture our non-monogamous relationship functioning?

- What level of transparency and communication do I expect from our other relationships?

- How much time and attention would you like us to allocate to our relationship compared to other partners?

- What are your feelings about meeting and interacting with each other's other partners (metamours)?

- Are there any specific relationship dynamics or labels you want to use or avoid (e.g., primary, secondary, nesting partner)?

- How would you like to handle conflicts or challenges that may arise within our non-monogamous relationship?

- How often should we have check-ins to discuss our feelings and experiences in the non-monogamous arrangement?

- What are your expectations regarding public displays of affection with other partners?

- What kind of support or reassurance would you like during changes or transitions within our relationships?

- Do you have any preferences or considerations about scheduling time with other partners and time spent together?

- What do you consider to be acceptable reasons for vetoing or ending a relationship with another partner?

- How can we ensure our non-monogamous lifestyle enhances and doesn't overshadow our overall relationship?

These are suggestions, and you may have yet to consider some of them, but they are all situations that require thought at some point along your journey. What better time to think about them than when creating your agreement?

Essential Things to Remember When Making a Relationship Agreement to Maintain Trust and Respect

- **Clear Communication**: Keep the conversations flowing like a well-oiled machine! Be open and honest with all partners at all times. Discuss any changes or adjustments to agreements and ensure everyone is informed and on board before acting on instincts or assumptions.

- **Consent and Informed Decision-making**: Ensure all partners consent to the relationship agreements. It's not enough to agree to something with your primary partner if your metamours are uncomfortable with the arrangement.

- **Responsibility and Accountability**: If you mess up, 'fess up. If you inadvertently breach an agreement, the first step is to admit where you went wrong and try to rectify the situation as soon as possible.

- **Avoid Assumptions**: Remember, you are not a mind-reader. If you aren't sure about something, ask for clarification rather than making assumptions about your partner's intentions or desires. To illustrate, 'sex' can mean different things for different people. Be specific about your agreement, and use direct language to define your terms. You can always change your relationship agreements if there's a mutual understanding, but mistakes will happen if people have different ideas about the ground rules.

- **Regular Check-Ins**: Schedule regular check-ins with all partners to discuss how the relationship agreements are being honored and if any adjustments are needed. Use these opportunities to ask each other how they feel about *everything*! Don't be scared to admit if things are not working as you'd hoped. The only way they can change is if you voice your thoughts.

- **Be Proactive**: Don't wait for the drama to come knocking; consider the potential challenges or conflicts and deal with them proactively. Discuss possible scenarios and how you can navigate them while respecting the relationship agreements. Your partner might be happy with a sexual act you are not okay with. Talk about ways you can accommodate everyone's needs in these situations, and aim to think about these scenarios before they are likely to occur.

- **Reevaluate and Adjust**: Be flexible, like a gymnast, and change agreements as the relationships evolve and your circumstances change. Many non-monogamous couples have commented that their original understanding was barely worth the paper it was written on because it was amended so quickly. Accept that things are likely to change all the time. Roll with the punches, and remember to enjoy the journey!

Dealing with Boundary Violations and Agreement Breakdowns

We've got to address the elephant in the room – what happens when our carefully crafted boundaries and agreements get violated? This can be a difficult conversation, but starting from a position of mutual respect is required, particularly in relationships with numerous partners. Ensure that the ground rules you lay out can be maintained by sticking to them and carrying through with the consequences if they are not.

It's like the fine print in a contract – not the fun part, but oh-so-necessary. Discussing what happens when we don't follow the rules might feel like a tricky chat, but remember, we're all in this together. Think of it as setting up a safety net in case one of you stumbles while juggling all those relationship balls.

It would help if you weren't too hard on each other when boundary violations occur, as it's integral to recognize that breakdowns can often happen, even in healthy relationships. We are all human, and often, breaches can happen due to distractions such as arguments or stressful issues at work.

Not all boundary breaches are done on purpose. Sometimes, it's a simple oversight, an emergency, or maybe they forgot a new rule.

Instead of getting upset or pointing the finger at your partner when a boundary has been unintentionally violated, address the situation promptly, calmly, and assertively. It's vital to address violations or agreement breakdowns as soon as possible, even though it might be uncomfortable. Letting them slide may lead to resentment from the partner who suggested the rule, and not enforcing the consequences as agreed will likely lead to further agreement-breaking.

Although it should not feel like school, this scenario is like teaching a child appropriate behaviors or manners. If you fail to establish consequences for poor behavior, the child will accept that there will be no repercussions, and the pattern of behavior will continue. In the same way, if your partner thinks you will let these things go, it negates the agreement's purpose.

Instead, address the issue calmly. If your partner forgets your "no texting other partner(s) during date nights" rule, avoid assuming they have ulterior motives and ask questions to clarify their intentions. They may have a valid reason, such as an emergency, or they may have forgotten what was agreed upon. Give them space and time to explain.

Be honest about how the violation has made you feel emotionally. Allow yourself to be vulnerable, but seek solutions rather than assigning blame. You may be outraged in the heat of the moment and need to request space and time before you can express your feelings in a non-emotive way. However, it is essential to acknowledge this to your partner so the situation is ultimately resolved rather than brushed under the carpet. Change your perceptions from negative to positive. Brainstorm possible resolutions together to prevent problems of this nature from occurring in the future and ensure you reestablish your boundaries. Reinforce your need to be heard so you know you are singing from the same music sheet.

Remember that revisiting and revising your agreement is ongoing as relationships evolve and you change and grow. A boundary established at the beginning of a relationship may not be relevant five years later—it may not even be relevant a month later! This is a voyage of discovery, and you should allow yourself some grace to tinker with the agreement until it feels right, at which point it will likely change again!

Try to maintain flexibility when adjusting your agreement according to your needs and changing circumstances. Both parties must understand that the goal is to be flexible *before* the boundary or pact is broken. Still, life is not always straightforward, and it is healthier to approach the issue from a place of curiosity rather than judgment.

Ask yourself how the violation makes you feel, and be honest about its effect. Do you know why you feel this way? How much did it alter your perspective and trust?

If a breach or breakdown of an agreement has damaged trust, both parties must cooperate to restore respect and foster conflict resolution through open communication and increased transparency. All boundaries must adhere to the relationship's values to build and maintain trust.

Just like a building needs a solid base to support the rest of the structure, so do relationships. If your relationship(s) aren't built on foundations of mutual understanding, openness, honesty, and trust, they have a higher chance of failing, even when you love your partner. This is why trust should be the main principle in your relationship(s).

Building Trust, Brick by Brick

Trust is like the comfy pillow that lets you sleep soundly when your partner is out and about. In non-monogamous relationships, where you are likely to have some feelings of insecurity, you need to be able to trust your partner to feel reassured. Trust is as vital for your mental health as it is for your physical well-being, and you must remember to take care of yourself and your partner(s).

To consciously build and maintain trust in non-monogamous relationships, agreements must be explicit, partners must check in regularly to renegotiate them as they evolve, and communication must be open, honest, and transparent. This might seem scary and overwhelming, but it doesn't need to be. If you check in regularly with each other, there is no reason why talking things through shouldn't get more manageable and, hopefully, more enjoyable as your journey evolves and grows!

Trust does not just break simply because a partner cheats. Trust can be damaged by repeating minor behaviors, such as a partner repeatedly breaking their word or telling white lies about where they have been, even if they weren't with other people. Sometimes, the small, day-to-day things have the most significant impact on the health of relationships. Building and maintaining trust in any relationship takes effort and sacrifice, but the complexities can seem more powerful in a non-monogamous arrangement.

The Foundation: Why Trust is Essential in Non-monogamy

Trust is the cornerstone of any non-monogamous relationship, and it holds even more weight than in monogamous relationships because of the added layers of complexity. There is a myth that people can't cheat in a non-monogamous relationship since they already have several partners. We have already explored why this isn't true, as we know that couples who enter into this lifestyle need to have explicit rules in place for it to work. Suppose a partner breaks the terms of an agreement, either because they failed to renegotiate a boundary before acting on their impulse or inadvertently broke trust through miscommunication or misunderstanding. In that case, rebuilding the trust they once had can be very difficult.

Trust allows a partner to feel comfortable, like a fluffy blanket, when their partner is out and about. This is vital in non-monogamous partnerships when people spend time with others. It is what enables people to communicate openly and freely. Without the right amount of trust, partners won't feel able to share their insecurities or have difficult conversations about their secret desires. Plus, it's vital for safe sex – because nobody wants surprises there.

Polyamorous relationships can involve several metamours, and everyone has to agree to and abide by the terms of your agreement. This sounds like a business agreement or contract, but it's supposed to be a lot more fun and freeing! In simple terms, establishing a framework means everyone can enjoy themselves and feel safe and secure at the same time.

Interestingly, many non-monogamous couples report meeting people who claim to be polyamorous but are actually in a monogamous relationship, and they do not feel brave enough to tell their partner they would like to explore an open relationship. They are then stuck in a situation where they either have to deny their true feelings, harbor resentment toward their partner, or have an affair. If the right amount of trust was in their original relationship, they might be brave enough to open up and communicate their feelings to their partner. Non-monogamy might not suit their partner's ideals, but expressing honest feelings is undoubtedly better than the hurt they will feel if they discover their partner is unfaithful further down the line.

Also, many couples choose poly/mono relationships, where one person in the primary relationship is polyamorous, and the other is strictly monogamous and is not interested in other relationships (which is 100% okay). In this scenario, check out Facebook support groups for advice. Ultimately, it's not a problem if one person wants to explore a non-monogamous relationship and the other doesn't. The same steps apply regarding boundaries, agreements, and rules. Trust is the key in this case (and all others, really).

Without trust, feelings of insecurity, jealousy, and fear can easily creep in and cause damage to the relationship. With trust, they can navigate non-monogamy complexities with confidence, emotional support, and a genuine sense of security. In contrast, the absence of trust can lead to emotional distress, conflicts, and barriers to personal and relational growth.

You might not trust a partner for many reasons; they do not have to be prominent. It could be as simple as telling you they would not be seen in public with a secondary partner (even if it doesn't appear romantic), but then a friend saw them together and messaged you about it.

Maybe it was their turn to cook dinner, and they forgot. If the little things become repeated problems, they will likely cause the first inklings of mistrust that can lead to more significant problems over time. It's a great idea to look at these minor issues while they are still small and talk to each other about how they make you feel and what can be done to fix them in a way that suits you both.

Trust isn't only about what your partner does (or doesn't do) - it also comes down to your perspective on what they did. If your partner sticks to their word and does what they say 95% of the time, but you make a big deal out of the 5%, feeling like they've broken your trust and let you down, you may need to look at the bigger picture. Are you turning a 5% fumble into a 100% catastrophe? In this moment, you and your partner can re-look and re-image your agreements (and possibly revisit your boundaries) to find ways that trust can be rebuilt constructively (no pun intended).

But here's the thing: trust only breaks if there are clear agreements and boundaries in the first place. If you never made an agreement for it, don't expect your partner to read your mind. Share your feelings, create agreements around it moving forward, and move on.

Jules, a 33-year-old blogger new to non-monogamy, has been in a relationship with Liam for almost two years. Jules loves going to the cinema, but their partner Liam has not suggested a movie date night. One day, they were walking through the mall and saw Liam with his secondary partner going to the cinema. They were pissed. When he got home that evening, Jules explained to Liam that they were hurt because he never goes to the cinema with them but takes his lover. He responded that he didn't know Jules enjoyed going to the movies, but now that he did, they could make it a date once a month. Jules agreed, releasing their anger and hurt because they understood it was a miscommunication and Liam didn't know.

Significant problems might be more readily apparent early on in the relationship. If a partner repeatedly fails to respect your boundaries, it may cause you stress and worry when they are seeing other people. How can you feel reassured if your partner has gone against your wishes before? Another potential red flag is finding yourself with a partner who attempts to cover certain behaviors. Suppose you meet someone who drinks a lot and has fewer inhibitions. You may feel concerned about whether or not they will be able to stick to the rules of the agreement, but you may also feel empathy and worry that they are unhappy. Many emotions can crop up, so discussing issues like this as and when they arise is essential to avoid further problems.

Without trust in the relationship, some couples go overboard with strict agreements, trying to control every move. However, this is not usually the best decision, as it can lead to feelings of suffocation and resentment. This can create a negative cycle of suspicion and conflict, which, over time, will erode emotional intimacy and promote hostility. Non-monogamous relationships that lack trust may reach a stalemate, where partners become so vulnerable that they stop communicating entirely, and renegotiation seems impossible.

The good news is that all of this is entirely avoidable if you keep talking to each other and practice effective listening. Be aware of each other's emotional insecurities and offer love and reassurance on difficult days. You might be pleasantly surprised when you realize that you share the same concerns as each other. Phew!

Building Blocks: Strategies for Building Trust

What we are about to tell you will probably not be shocking, yet it's important enough to mention. Before reading the subsequent few sentences, take a deep breath and ask yourself: Do I wholeheartedly practice this?

Okay, here we go...

The first strategy for building trust is to have open and honest communication: this means learning how to express your feelings, needs, and concerns freely and listening to your partner in return.

But before you even get to this step, there's a secret "step zero" – being honest with yourself. Yeah, that's right, you gotta figure out what's going on inside your own head first. When you can be aware of your own feelings, needs, and concerns, then and only then can you learn to share them with others. This is easier for some than others, but it is necessary in a non-monogamous arrangement, and, like anything else, we promise it gets easier with practice!

For instance, if you're feeling insecure about a new partner your primary partner is seeing, it is much healthier to voice your feelings instead of keeping them bottled up. If you're not careful, those bottled emotions will eventually explode like a shaken soda can. Compressing and sitting on your true feelings will ultimately affect your mental health, happiness, and trust. It would help if you allowed yourself to be vulnerable with your partner so they could help you work through these emotions. Nobody is a mind reader, and while they might be able to tell from your body language that you are anxious, they might not know why you feel the way you do. Talk to them! They probably feel much the same as you do!

The second secret ingredient in our trust-building recipe is discipline, with a capital "D." Discipline in non-monogamous relationships is crucial for creating a stable, respectful, and trusting environment. It means sticking to your agreements, practicing emotional control (no Hulk moments, please), being honest, and showing empathy for your partner(s). Discipline can help you grow and strengthen your non-monogamous relationship by building trust and emotional security. It might sound like a lot of work, but think of it as flexing your relationship muscles – the more you do it, the stronger your relationship gets. Clarifying your needs and desires when renegotiating agreements will simplify this process.

When working on trust in your relationships, you need to prioritize consistency and reliability. When you say you will pick your partner up from work, ensure you turn up on time (kudos for being a bit early with a big smile). Follow through on agreements to demonstrate you are trustworthy and show your partner that they are important enough to you to do your best for them. Most people actively want to be in their partner's good books. Investing in your relationship can only strengthen your bond.

As stated before, you can only control yourself and what you do and say. Trust can be tricky when it comes to control, especially when you're in a non-monogamous relationship because trust doesn't only include you and your partner but also your secondary partners, your partner's secondary partners, and the world as a whole. When you trust the world and those around you, you'll have more faith in yourself and your partner. This trust forms the foundation for building agreements and navigating the complexities of a non-monogamous relationship.

The thing about building trust is that it's not just about boundaries and agreements (and sticking to them). It's also about commitment and, more importantly, values. In the cake of life, limits, arrangements, and dedication form the cake sponge, but values are the icing - you've got something decent without it, and you'll eat it if there are no other treats in the house... but when you add the icing, you elevate the cake, take it to the next level of yummy. This is the same in relationships.

Values are pivotal in shaping the foundation of trust within a relationship, as they provide a shared framework that guides behavior, communication, and decision-making. Values are the goals that motivate you in life, and they can be anything from loyalty and charity to honesty and spiritualism. When we choose partners with values that align with our own, we limit misunderstandings while creating a deep sense of reliability and predictability (not in a boring way, but in a trust-creating way). These shared values serve as a roadmap for each partner's actions, making it more likely that their choices will resonate with their partner's desires and expectations.

Plus, sharing values with your partner(s) allows for open communication and transparency, establishing a deeper understanding. When you understand why your partner does what they do, you'll see their sincerity and genuineness shining through. Open and honest conversations are great for understanding each other's aspirations, goals, boundaries, and priorities. And when it comes to transparency, talk is not cheap; it's more precious than gold and diamonds.

You can supercharge trust by investing time and effort in emotional intimacy. It's like planting trust seeds that'll grow into a trusty trust tree. Talk to your partner(s) about how they like to receive love and affection. The 5 Love Languages—physical touch, words of affirmation, quality time, receiving gifts, and acts of service—are a great place to start building emotional intimacy.[48]

Enjoying shared experiences allows you and your partner(s) to create shared memories and intense bonds. Want to go on a hot air balloon? Please do it! Feel like having a picnic on the beach at sunset? Awesome. Find things you and your partner(s) want to do specific to each other and savor that time-building closeness.

Lastly, throw in some regular reassurance and check-ins to let your partner(s) know they're loved and valued. Discuss feelings and experiences during your check-ins to address any concerns openly. Remember to address areas of conflict rationally and calmly and seek to find resolutions rather than calling out your inner drama queen to play.

Repairing Cracks: Rebuilding Trust After It's Been Broken

Repairing trust often feels as challenging as trying to piece together a shattered vase; it's tedious and frustrating. However, in Chinese culture, they mend these broken vases using not just ordinary glue but precious gold, enhancing their value. Similarly, our relationships can undergo a transformation, becoming even more precious and resilient when trust is rebuilt with care and commitment.

In their podcast, *A Touch of Flavor*, Josh and Cassie[49] look at how trust can be rebuilt after it has been broken. Josh acknowledges that it requires courage and is a challenging process that many find difficult, but asserts that it ultimately begins with the decision to move forward honestly with a promise that you will never break the rules again. He says if the desire to stop hurting your partner isn't there, the relationship will probably not work. Heart-wrenching stuff!

Having integrity in your relationships is the bread and butter of success. Integrity is integral to the foundation you build in your partnerships to make them fulfilling and healthy.

While deciding not to breach an agreement ever again is healthy, this is a lot of pressure to put on an open relationship. Moving from monogamy to non-monogamy could feel like being a kid in a candy shop with tons of new candy options. You've always had Snickers, but now you can't stop drooling over the Kit-Kats, M&Ms, and, oh my gosh, is that Hershey's?! This is why it's necessary to be able to rearrange the agreements from time to time (*before* trying out the new candies). This gives the extra-excited partner who wishes to try all the sweets in one purchase (instead of multiple slow and steady purchases) the opportunity to have a little fun, too.

So, when those candy-loving impulses get the best of you and break an agreement (or you *think* it does), it's crucial to acknowledge the breach, understand the impact, and apologize sincerely. Remember, you are in a relationship, which means other people's emotions are involved. What you do doesn't just affect you but also the others in the relationship.

Although this requires courage and may result in an emotional response from both parties, it is an excellent idea to adopt a 'Zero Hiding Policy' as part of your agreement. It is up to you and your partner to determine an arrangement that works best for you, but putting your cards on the table and being completely honest is undoubtedly the quickest path to resolution. Try to resist the temptation to tell half-truths to absolve yourself of responsibility and protect your partner's feelings. If you can hold up your hands and admit you are wrong, you are far more likely to rebuild trust than if they discover what happened later. Let everything out. They will be hurt, and there may be anger, but this is the first step to moving forward together.

Be sincere in your apology and accept accountability. This is an excellent way to express your commitment to honesty and respect and is a valid reminder that you are only human and we all make mistakes. There is a lot to think about in some agreements, and there are bound to be a few ups and downs as you learn to navigate the challenges of your new lifestyle. Be kind to each other, and do your best to take the necessary steps to resolve the problem as quickly as possible to avoid prolonged secrecy.

If your partner agrees, explore the reasons behind the breach together. Discuss why it happened and prevent those candy-loving impulses from causing future mishaps.

Minor mistakes can rock the boat, and you must reassure your partner of your dedication to the relationship and your desire to do better to rebuild trust. Allowing your partner the space and time to deal with what happened would be best. Practice the art of patience while they are healing.

Talk about ways you both feel you can move forward. Discuss setting new boundaries or ensuring agreements are honored from now on. Talk to each other about the lessons you have learned from this issue, and be frank about how you can grow from it to strengthen the relationship from now on.

The feelings may be a little more complicated for the person whose trust has been broken, but there are strategies you can employ to work your way through the negative emotions you may be feeling.

Consistency and reliability solidify trust. Being honest in your words and consistent in your actions shows your partner that they can rely on you. If you promise to text your partner before going on a date with someone else, consistently follow through with this promise to show your partner they can trust you to respect their needs.

Repairing trust takes time and consistent effort. It's essential to show through your actions that you're committed to change, but it can be achieved with the right attitude and approach. Over time, you can gradually rebuild trust by consistently respecting boundaries and being open and honest; the experience may improve your relationship.

Navigating & Balancing Multiple Relationships

Non-monogamous relationships present unique challenges, often taking people by surprise when they embark on this journey. In his 2021 article on this subject, Forest Williams says that bringing monogamous attitudes into non-monogamous relationships is one of the biggest mistakes made by people new to this lifestyle. Approaching non-monogamy the same way you came to your monogamous relationship is like trying to play basketball with a fishing rod.[50] He likens the different relationship formats to games with various rules. You are playing a new game, and it will take time to learn the rules. Two of the big rules are learning how to handle relationship transitions and how to balance multiple partners.

In this chapter, we will look at the hurdles of both while maintaining the integrity of your relationships during these shifts.

The Ebb and Flow: Understanding Common Relationship Transitions

Change should be embraced or avoided, depending on your personality type. Those who embark on non-monogamous relationships are arguably more willing to embrace change than those who rely on the predictable safety net and, dare we say, the monotony of their monogamous lifestyle. Fortune favors the bold, and those willing to open their relationships to find their authentic selves, as opposed to society's ideals of exclusivity, could be rewarded with a greater sense of trust, freedom, excitement, sexual fulfillment, and fresh energy in their partnerships.

While the scope and scale of change can be a little overwhelming in a non-monogamous relationship, a recent journal article published in Sexual and Relationship Therapy conducted with older, non-monogamous adults suggests that the participants were "happier, healthier, and more sexually active than the general population of similar age and relationship status."[51]

However, it can be a challenging road to this haven of joy. Change can occur often and prove difficult to manage in open relationships. When you let down your guard and let others in, you are met with many new experiences. While exciting and liberating, new sexual partners, new relationships, changing commitments, and the end of relationships can feel overwhelming.

When you're recalibrating your heart and hormones to this new reality, feeling like a fish out of water is perfectly normal. If you and your partner have been in a relatively stable and long-term relationship, dealing with the often dynamic shifts that open connections present can be quite a shock.

Examples of these are as follows:

- New partners.

- Partners leaving.

- Changes in relationship hierarchy, such as a non-monogamous individual dating someone new or a partner ending a relationship, have a ripple effect on everyone involved.

- Change to a non-hierarchical structure where no primary partnership exists, and all parties are considered equal.

Unlike the stability you have come to expect from an exclusive, monogamous relationship, non-monogamous relationships can be fluid and continuously changing. Not only do people change all the time as they experience new things and grow, but the relationship will always be in flux as you add more people into the mix.

So, how do you handle the overwhelm?

When life throws you a relationship curveball, take a deep breath and give yourself and your partner time to process each new change and desire. It's good to accept that this will occasionally happen, especially in the early days.

Also, don't let those pesky insecurities buzz around your head like a swarm of overly enthusiastic bees. This isn't a rejection party; it's a conversation. Your partner's openness is a testament to their affection for you, a declaration that they're committed to finding a way for you both to continue this unique journey together.

Flexibility, Adaptability, and Humanity

In ethical non-monogamous relationships, change is a constant companion. As individuals grow and evolve, so do their connections. Whether it's deepening feelings, the renegotiation of boundaries, or shifts in personal circumstances, being prepared for these natural evolutions is essential.

Instead of approaching change with trepidation or resistance, consider it an opportunity for profound growth and an avenue to fortify your connections further. Embracing change within ethical non-monogamy can lead to deeper understanding, enhanced communication, and a more profound sense of intimacy among all involved parties. That's why it's crucial to remember that every person your partner may be dating or that you may be dating is just that—a person. Each individual deserves love, respect, and consideration just as much as you do.

This fundamental recognition of the humanity of all involved parties lies at the heart of accepting flexibility and adaptability in this journey. When you approach your partners and their connections with the understanding that they are unique individuals with their own desires, emotions, and needs, you cultivate a culture of empathy and compassion. This perspective helps you navigate change and shifting dynamics with greater ease because you honor the humanity of those involved.

Now, let's delve into the fascinating concept of New Relationship Energy (NRE) to prepare for its emergence when someone else joins the relationship train.

New Relationship Energy (NRE)

New Relationship Energy (NRE) is the way non-monogamous people define those early days in a relationship that are filled with excitement, lust, and desire. NRE is the electric connection you share with someone who desires you as much as you desire them. It's what monogamous couples might call the honeymoon period, when the happy chemicals in your brain are soaring. NRE is when we see only the positives in a new love interest before considering anything negative.

The Positives of NRE:

- An increase in levels of dopamine and norepinephrine in the limbic system. These are nature's "feel-good" stimulants. Activity increases in the parts of your brain involved in arousal and pleasure.

- When this happens, people tend to shut out the rest of the world to devote themselves to their new connections. In a monogamous relationship, this would undoubtedly be a very positive thing. It can still be viewed as a positive thing in non-monogamous relationships, but when others are involved, you must remember to exercise caution. At this point, the hormones coursing through your body affect your judgment. It's a beautiful, exciting, and dangerous feeling. You feel alive and so happy to have a new mutual connection. Run with it and enjoy it, but remember to think about how it might affect the other people in your relationship.

- One of the benefits of open relationships is the ability to experience NRE without ending an existing relationship. This means you can encounter this feeling over and over again.

The Negatives of NRE:

- One of the cons of NRE is that some partners can feel neglected. You may forget prior commitments and wish to spend time with the new partner. Although you may Netflix and Chill with your "old" partner, now you wish to do similar or the same activities with the "new" partner. Keep your other partners in mind as you navigate these muddy waters. How may they be feeling throughout this change? Balancing the excitement of a fresh connection with the ongoing commitment to your existing relationships is the real art of managing NRE.

- The intensity of desire can lead to impulsive decisions, breaking agreements and boundaries in a frenzy of emotional highs. This can lead to misunderstandings, hurt feelings, and even conflicts within your other relationships.

- Another con is avoiding red flags and putting this new partner on a pedestal in your head. When new relationships have yet to develop, you can't be sure what impact they might have on your life. Your primary partner may be second on your list of priorities when you are in the moment and deeply in lust with someone new.

- In the world of NRE, it's easy to forget that your primary partner has been your rock, your confidant, and your partner-in-crime long before this new character entered the scene. So, while it's exhilarating to ride the rollercoaster of NRE, remember that your primary partner is the one who helped build the theme park in the first place. Balancing your affection between the old and the new can be challenging but worth mastering.

- With open relationships, you enjoy the feeling of NRE repeatedly, but you will likely experience the end of relationships more frequently.

For the partner experiencing NRE:
- No matter what, stick to your relationship agreements. Suppose you sense that you are proceeding in a direction where you need to change a relationship agreement; speak about it *beforehand*, not afterward. By maintaining honesty with your partner and giving them time to process all these new feelings, you are honoring your commitments and building trust with your current partners as you allow the NRE feeling to grow organically. Slow down and let your existing partner(s) get used to the idea. There is no rush. Enjoy

the journey because waiting sometimes makes a good thing even better!

- The reason why it is so important to discuss changes to your agreement before acting on them is to put yourself in your partner's shoes. Imagine a scenario where your partner comes home and says, "I had unsafe sex with them. Sorry, I know I broke an agreement, but now I want to have a relationship with them." If that scenario triggers any emotions in you, remember that your partner might feel the same way if the roles were reversed.

- Reassure your partner that you still love them and are here for them. Remind them of your love and commitment to your existing relationship(s). You've chosen to embark on this journey together, not so you can run off with someone new, but to experience the upsides together. Even the most solid of relationships can get wobbly when encountering new people. Tell your partner how much they mean to you, and remember why you are doing this.

- Introducing a new player into the relationship can alter the dynamics. Re-negotiate boundaries, time management, and any other concerns with your partners. Make sure everyone's on the same page and agrees to the new arrangement.

- Remind yourself that it is paramount to be aware of your euphoria and that "This too shall pass." Enjoy it to the fullest, but also remember your prior commitments to other relationships that may not be feeling the NRE.

- Learn to channel your newfound love and energy to everyone's advantage. Spread the love, not just among your new connections. Utilize those good feelings to benefit ALL of your partnerships and commitments.

- Be conscious of and sensitive to the feelings of your partner(s). Remember that the arrival of a new love interest on the scene has a ripple effect and might affect other partners and your primary partner. Communication and consideration are your allies here.

- Don't make significant life decisions in the throes of NRE. If you act on it in haste, this will be very detrimental to your other long-term relationships. Remember how you felt about your partner when you first got together, and it was about lovely meals, exciting sex, and mini breaks? It is easy to forget all that when washing their underwear and wishing they wouldn't clip their toenails in the living room. Remember that life together might not be as exhilarating and glamorous as it was in the early days, but you wouldn't be here if you didn't love and respect that person.

- Regular check-ins are crucial during this stage. Schedule open and honest discussions about your experiences, emotions, and uncertainties. Ask your partner how they are feeling, and listen to their concerns. Check-in with your values: Is this new person supporting your shared mission and vision? Look at the partnership and ask yourself if it benefits everyone.

For the partners of a partner with NRE:
- Take deep breaths. This stage is challenging, but so are you. You wouldn't have come this far if you weren't. Trust in the process, but allow yourself to feel and accept what you feel. The key to maintaining your sanity is patience. Repeat this mantra as needed—NRE is about the chemicals in their brain going haywire, not a commentary on your worth or relationship. This, too, shall pass.

- Allow the person in the NRE phase to ride it out, but warn them against making significant decisions now. They likely won't want to listen to any negatives, but a gentle reminder that they have prior commitments and not to neglect those commitments might be warranted.

- If you see a red flag from the metamour or your partner, it's okay to call it out. This should be included in your agreement anyway. In the same way that some partners have safe words or can veto certain people, this is an excellent point to have in there somewhere.

- Try to be busy while your partner is on a date rather than worrying the whole time. Enjoy your extra alone time, plan in advance to work on a specific project, or find your own new relationship to enjoy.

- Scheduled check-ins with your partner are essential. Use these opportunities to share your feelings, address concerns, and reaffirm your love and commitment. Talking openly can be quite a complex process for people in the early stages of their ethical non-monogamy journey, but this is not the time to be a closed book. Expressing your positive and negative feelings means that everyone understands what is going well and what needs a spot of revisiting.

- Another positive way to remind yourself why you are doing this is to celebrate one another's successes and support each other when things get challenging. Imagine that you might want to practice the art of compersion. This might be tricky to get your head around, but practice makes perfect! Learning to feel happy for your partner when they have a great date will reassure them, and sharing their excitement for their new relationship involves your ever-expanding happiness.

- Likewise, offering support to your partner when they have a date that didn't go to plan can also be a positive reminder that you are always there for each other, even when you aren't together, further maintaining trust by creating a safe space where you can all express your feelings, emotions, fears, joys, and needs.

Balancing Multiple Partners

To truly delve into the intricate world of ethical non-monogamy, one must start with a fundamental truth: relationships are not static entities but rather ever-evolving, dynamic forces. Each connection, as unique as a fingerprint, carries its own set of desires, needs, and boundaries. Imagine this as the challenge of taming a multi-headed dragon, where each head symbolizes a separate connection within the intricate web of love.

This complexity arises from the interplay of emotions, time, and resources. It's vital to recognize that investing time and energy in one partner doesn't diminish your love or commitment to another. Instead, it underscores the importance of actively managing these finite resources to meet the emotional and physical needs of all parties involved.

Balancing multiple relationships demands meticulous time management, much like conducting a symphony. The crux is allocating time based on each partner's unique needs and your thoughtful agreements. Some relationships may demand more attention due to their intensity or circumstances, while others thrive with less. Finding equilibrium is the secret to nurturing everyone involved.

This balance is achieved through weaving clear boundaries and fostering open communication with all parties. Regular check-ins serve as your compass, ensuring their needs are met, concerns addressed, and conflicts resolved. These conversations are the building blocks of trust, which is the bedrock of ethical non-monogamy.

As relationships evolve, so do the agreements that govern them. Agreements regarding time spent together, date nights, and even fluid-bonding practices may shift as mutual partnerships are formed or transform. These shifts don't signal instability but rather reflect the dynamic nature of human connections. Open dialogue is the key here, as partners' needs and comfort levels may evolve, necessitating discussions about boundaries, sexual health practices, and time allocation.

In the world of ethical non-monogamy, love knows no bounds, yet time and energy remain finite resources. Managing these resources effectively, much like tending to a diverse garden of plants, each with distinct needs, ensures every relationship thrives.

Indeed, no two connections are alike; they are masterpieces shaped by unique individuals, histories, desires, and the mutual agreements forged. This recognition of diversity is the cornerstone of thriving in ethical non-monogamy, where you cultivate a garden of enriching, harmonious relationships, each as unique and vibrant as the next.

Maintaining Relationship Integrity

Relationship transitions and the balancing act of having multiple partners can be challenging, but they also offer opportunities for growth and deepening connections. For example, in an interview with Us Weekly, Will Smith and Jada Pinkett-Smith confirmed their open relationship had stopped their marriage from feeling like a prison and had given them trust and freedom. When Smith opened up about their non-monogamous relationship following allegations that his wife had been unfaithful, he was very candid about the fact that this arrangement had enabled them to support one another unconditionally, which, to them, was the highest definition of love.[52]

The post-transition stage of a relationship can bring partners closer once they have successfully navigated a trying time. The next chapter will focus on how a non-monogamous lifestyle can lead to personal growth, self-discovery, fulfillment, happiness, and satisfaction.

Embracing the Personal Growth Journey

This chapter isn't just a one-time read. It's your anchor to return to whenever doubt creeps in. Non-monogamy is about building a life that fits you, not just your partner(s). You deserve to find your happiness, growth, and meaning within it. So whenever you feel adrift, flip back to this chapter and let it remind you of why you started this journey in the first place.

The transformative power of embracing non-monogamy extends far beyond the realm of relationships. Those who have ventured down this path often find themselves on an incredible journey of self-discovery and personal growth. With honesty and transparency at its core, non-monogamy offers a resilience that sets it apart from its monogamous counterpart. The liberation accompanying open communication can be nothing short of profound, with some individuals even uncovering a sense of spiritual enlightenment through these unconventional relationships.

However, it's understandable that the idea of moving away from a monogamous relationship can be daunting. Fear of failure might be knocking at your door, but remember, it's easier to stick to the same old, even if it's about as exciting as watching paint dry. But we find personal growth and meaning when we take risks and try new things. While non-monogamy may come with challenges, the rewards can be life-altering. Don't let fear hold you back from exploring all life's possibilities.

Stepping Outside Your Comfort Zone

Stepping outside our comfort zones allows us to test our limits, conquer our fears, and discover hidden talents or passions that can lead to a more fulfilling life. While safety provides stability, it can also breed stagnation and predictability. When we constantly seek security, we may miss out on opportunities for adventure, personal development, and meaningful connections with others. Embracing discomfort and uncertainty can lead to a more vibrant life, where true happiness is found in the exhilaration of taking chances and embracing the unknown. So call in your inner lotus flower and be ready to bloom in muddy waters.

Abigail Brenner explains that stepping outside our comfort zone is essential for growth, with five significant benefits.[53] They are:

1. **Real life awaits:** Beyond fear lies a world of experiences, both favorable and challenging, that beckon us to become the best versions of ourselves.

2. **Find your inner power:** Challenging our limits reveals our untapped resourcefulness and capabilities, proving that we are more resilient and resourceful than we often believe.

3. **Personal growth:** Risks are the stepping stones to growth, with mistakes serving as valuable lessons. Shifting our perspective transforms "FAIL" into "First Attempt In Learning" and "FEAR" into "Face Everything And Rise."

4. **Self-discovery:** Settling for mediocrity and misery is a considerable price to avoid stepping out of your comfort zone. Experiences make us learn and develop life skills and self-discovery. Braving new things expands the size of your comfort zone as new things quickly become familiar.

5. **Embrace change:** Confronting the unknown equips us with the tools to navigate life's tran-

sitions effectively. With every life transition, you improve, and with every experience, you become more resilient and better able to cope.

If you are still reading at this point, it's safe to say that you have chosen the non-monogamy relationship style (and are probably in the midst of its ups and downs). This will not always be easy, but the rewards may outweigh the difficulties. Please be patient, and keep reminding yourself that your journey will differ from that of others embarking on the same voyage of discovery. But if you never try, you will never know.

As you continue your expedition into non-monogamy, remember that personal development is not a destination but a continuous process. Every interaction, challenge, and emotion present an opportunity for learning and growth. As you evolve, so does your resilience, sharpening your emotional intelligence and enhancing your understanding of yourself and your partner(s).

Developing Emotional Intelligence

Kendra Cherry defines Emotional Intelligence (EI), also known as Emotional Quotient (EQ), as "the ability to perceive, interpret, demonstrate, control, evaluate, and use emotions to communicate with and relate to others effectively and constructively." Experts suggest that high

Emotional Intelligence is more important than cognitive intelligence (IQ) in determining happiness and success. [54]

While a high IQ might land you a job, your EQ is your ticket to success in every corner of your life and the key to tackling stress and challenges. As your IQ helps you with calculations, EQ measures your emotional competence, empathy, and knack for navigating the turbulent waters of human interaction.

Non-monogamy requires nimble emotional footwork, self-awareness, and top-notch communication skills. By engaging in this lifestyle, you are already adopting and refining your emotional intelligence all the time, and this can actively help you with all of your relationships. You don't need to be an EQ guru from the get-go; you'll grow over time as you consciously strive to be a better human for yourself and your partners.

By developing our emotional intelligence, we can increase our happiness and satisfaction. To build our emotional intelligence, we need to find ways to control our own emotions in times of chaos, but we also need to learn the importance of empathy and understand how to respond appropriately to the emotional needs of others.

There are four steps to emotional intelligence, which become more complex as you work from 1 to 4: [55]

1. **Perceiving emotions:** The ability to perceive emotions by developing an awareness of non-ver-

bal cues, like the raised eyebrow or the suppressed smile. Recognizing the facial expressions and body language of your partner(s) to understand how they are feeling accurately.

2. **Reasoning with emotions:** Little by little, you start understanding why you react the way you do to certain situations and what triggers those emotional responses.

3. **Understanding emotions:** Emotions can be complicated regarding how they make us react and how others perceive them. For example, if your partner expresses angry feelings, you must learn how to read them, as they could be interpreted differently. Are they unhappy about something you have done, or are they deflecting their anger because they just received a parking ticket?

4. **Managing emotions:** This is the highest level of Emotional intelligence, as it is the trickiest to control. Learning to regulate your emotions, responding appropriately no matter how you feel, and remaining empathetic to the feelings of others is a skill that requires practice and refinement.

We can work on Emotional Intelligence by focusing on our feelings and building self-awareness. Journaling can be an effective way to observe your feelings. Becoming more self-aware may help you become more open-minded and less judgmental. Spending time focusing on areas where you are lacking will make you more considerate of others' feelings. Put yourself in their shoes and try to imagine how they are feeling. Mindfulness is another way to develop our EQ by encouraging ourselves to learn to be in the present moment and not dwell on the past or future.

Signs of Emotional Intelligence are:

- An awareness of personal strengths and weaknesses.

- Self-confidence, acceptance, and the ability to let go of mistakes.

- The ability to perceive and describe how someone else is feeling through their words and non-verbal cues.

- Accepting and embracing change.

- Feeling concern, empathy, and sensitivity toward others.

- Accepting accountability for your actions.

- Your emotions stay steady during stormy times.

Non-monogamy turbocharges your emotional intelligence journey. With multiple partners, you become a pro at reading body language and non-verbal cues, understanding why we and our partners feel the way we do, and learning to regulate how we respond to these situations through communication and empathy.

Jeanne Segal, Ph.D., argues that refining our emotional intelligence isn't just beneficial; it's downright essential [56] It deepens your understanding of relationships, helps you navigate emotional minefields, and empowers you to address issues before they become relationship wreckers.

Embracing Authenticity

When our actions and words are misaligned, we hinder our growth and cheat ourselves and those around us. Living an authentic life is an ongoing process; like peeling back the layers of an onion, we learn more about ourselves through life experiences.[57]

In the quest for authentic living, aligning our lifestyle with our deepest values and desires, including non-monogamy, is paramount. No one should settle for the mold society attempts to impose upon them. You are your own compass, and you know what brings you happiness, regardless of societal conditioning. That flicker of self-acceptance is a step toward proving that love and happiness come in diverse forms, each tailored to the individual.

Don't let societal stereotypes rain on your parade. If anything, let them fuel your resolve to show naysayers that alternative paths exist and can be way more fun. No one should feel compelled to live a falsehood for the sake of others' comfort. True satisfaction and fulfillment can only be found in authenticity. Being authentic in your relationships makes you a good role model for others with the same thought processes. Not only will it help them to express their own authenticity, but over time, it will also help society as a whole to reassess their opinions surrounding this lifestyle choice.

Breaking free from the expectations imposed by others, even when you believe you know your heart's desires, can be a formidable challenge. In her recent article, Liz Sinclair[58] explains that her non-monogamy journey developed from a purely physical need to a more authentic experience through personal growth. She states that it's about more than sex. It's a journey of discovering sexuality, sensuality, needs, desires, and wants. This personal growth allows for authentic living.

Author Oonagh Sullivan[59] describes authenticity as being absolutely vital in non-monogamy. She says authenticity is the foundation of ethical non-monogamy. It's a pillar of healthy relationships where we feel safe enough to be entirely and authentically loved. Avoiding conflict in certain relationships means we deny some truths about what we want and who we are. We deny others the opportunity to make us feel more loved and seen, ultimately perpetuating the belief that we're not worthy of being loved as we are, or if we're our true selves, we'll be rejected or abandoned.

Non-monogamy provides people with the opportunity to explore the capacity to love more than one person, the ability to fulfill their sexual desires, and the chance to let their authentic selves shine like a disco ball at a '70s dance party. When we embrace authenticity, we allow ourselves to experience different types of love and relationships, with the understanding that love is inexhaustible and that loving multiple people concurrently does not diminish the love we feel for each individual within the relationship.

The need for open communication and honesty in non-monogamous relationships can lead to greater openness and transparency when discussing needs. This deeper connection will lead to a stronger sense of shared values and increased trust and intimacy, giving non-monogamous partnerships stronger bonds, significant overall happiness, and maximum fulfillment. The success of non-monogamous relationships is a life lesson for society and another step towards acceptance.

Learning to Love More

Non-monogamy is a classroom for expanding your heart's capacity and rewiring your perspective on love. It challenges the traditional view that love must be confined to a single container, showing that your heart can stretch and bend to include a wide range of connections. By embracing multiple connections, you experience firsthand that love isn't a finite resource but an abundant, boundless, and renewable energy.

As you navigate diverse relationships, you learn to appreciate each unique bond and recognize that there's always room for more love in your life. This variety reinforces the idea that love is not limited by quantity but enriched by diversity. Your relationships, whether romantic, platonic, or everything in between, contribute to your emotional growth and understanding.

Non-monogamy becomes a transformative journey that dissolves the scarcity mindset and reveals the endless horizons of love's potential. It's reminding you that your heart is not a confined space but a universe waiting to be explored. Non-monogamy is like boldly going where no heart has gone before. It's Captain Kirk navigating the love-iverse, discovering new galaxies of emotions, and beaming up love connections like they're dilithium crystals.

Every connection you foster reinforces the idea that love knows no borders. This perspective seeps into other areas of your life, enriching your relationships, self-perception, and ability to give and receive affection. In the grand classroom of non-monogamy, you learn that the more you love, the more love you have to offer, and the richer life becomes.

Growing Through Challenges

While we accept that non-monogamy presents some reasonably hefty challenges, these offer excellent opportunities for personal growth. For example, some people may find compersion – that warm, fuzzy feeling when your partner finds another lover – as easy as pie. In contrast, others may discover it to be a rather grueling process of battling innate jealousy and insecurity until it starts feeling more normal. It takes resilience to deprogram our mind and body's natural stress responses and work through these emotions until we reach the other side. This can be a very trying journey. However, it forces us to self-analyze, ask ourselves some searching questions, and re-think some of the 'truths' we once believed.

During the most demanding challenges, we experience significant growth, expand our minds, and learn who we are. Yes, there will be some unpleasant emotions to navigate through in the beginning, but once you have learned to recognize that, even the jealousy you feel can be considered healthy and may even promote the fuel for desire when you reconnect with your partner after a date with someone else.

Managing multiple relationships, even consensually, can present unexpected challenges. Your calendar may look like a Tetris game on steroids, fitting in dates, check-ins, and quality time with partners. You may find that much of your free time is lost to meeting the needs of others, and making time to check in with partners removes a lot of the alone time you used to enjoy. By maintaining open lines of communication, these concerns can be expressed early so that everyone in the relationship can find methods that work for them to overcome any issues before they take hold. Whether or not you are consciously aware of it, regular communication devoted to problem-solving and ironing out anxieties makes you more adept at expressing your needs and leads to personal growth.

You might not realize it, but every time you successfully work through a challenge in your non-monogamous relationships, you teach yourself valuable life skills about conflict resolution and negotiation. You will learn how to be a better communicator and listener. These skills will spill over into other areas of your life positively, increasing your confidence and boosting your resilience.

Expanding Your Worldview

In the Western world, society is mono-normative, meaning that the cultural view is still very much in favor of monogamy. However, in other countries, they do not appear to have such qualms. In Kenya's Masaai tribes, polygamy is widely accepted, with men paying their wives for cows.[60] Non-monogamous relationships are more financially viable in farming regions of Nepal, where fraternal polyandry used to be commonplace. This meant a woman would marry several brothers simultaneously so that there were more hands to help cultivate the land.[61] In Tibet, polyandry is the unspoken norm, and many women cannot be sure who fathered their children.[62] In poorer places, polyamorous relationships are more a measure of financial sensibility than a lifestyle choice. Western society is far from enlightened, but non-monogamy is no new idea.

We have established that humans can love more than one person and that doing so can be an infinitely rewarding experience. Loving several people from different backgrounds can shine a light on foreign cultures, religions, and people's spiritual views and ways of life. You will experience a diverse and rich mix of opinions and perspectives, broadening your horizons and making you more well-rounded and open-minded. You will also learn a great deal from talking to different people.

Meeting people from different walks of life may introduce you to new hobbies and teach you a great deal about things you may never encounter with only one partner. Not only will your life become more fulfilling and enriched, but your entire outlook on life and the values you held previously could change with access to a mixed bag of different perspectives.

By embarking on a journey of non-monogamy, you will also open up your life to a vast community of other like-minded people. This, in turn, will expand your social circle even more and increase your confidence as you develop a greater sense of belonging.

Hopefully, you now have a better idea about the benefits of embracing the authentic lifestyle you deserve without fear or judgment. In the conclusion, we will recap everything we have covered and learn how to continue exploring this remarkable journey.

Conclusion

You've reached the end of your crash course on non-monogamy and all the weird and enticing elements that come with it. We hope you have found this book informative and helpful on your journey. Now, you can see the many positives such a lifestyle offers anyone who feels the time has come for their relationship(s) to evolve differently.

Monogamy is not for everyone, and even though society dictates that we all fit the same mold, we all have unique needs and desires, and we should be allowed to express these freely without inhibitions. We should not have to seek permission to love more than one person.

We hope to have given you a greater understanding of the road ahead and that you feel excited and empowered to explore this voyage of self-discovery without fear or anxiety. The rewards are abundant when you acknowledge your truth and embrace the benefits of multiple partners in your life.

Whenever the journey gets bumpy, use this as your guide. Seek solace by revisiting the sections of this book that offer the guidance that is the most relevant to you. Always remember that you are not alone.

In our journey into non-monogamy, we looked at the following:

- Chapter 1 explored what non-monogamy is and debunked the associated myths. We looked at societal stigma and examined methods to navigate negative responses.

- Chapter 2 discussed why monogamy isn't for everyone and explored the benefits of non-monogamous partnerships. We considered why it might be the right lifestyle choice for you.

- Chapter 3 evaluated the intricate aspects of the transition to non-monogamy and the difficulties you may experience. We looked at the potential impacts on mental health, and how to comprehend the associated anxieties and jealousies we may feel in the initial stages of a non-monogamous lifestyle.

- Chapter 4 covered our emotional and physical well-being and the importance of making time for self-care. We considered support systems and looked at developing individual, non-monogamous toolkits to support us on our journey.

- Chapter 5 focused on the importance of open and honest communication and transparency in non-monogamous relationships. We scoured ways to navigate difficult conversations and the art of compassionate communication, along with tips on overcoming difficulties you may encounter.

- Chapter 6 discussed the importance of setting boundaries and agreements within non-monogamous relationships. We covered the need for regular communication to ensure everyone is on the same page and feels secure enough in the relationship to express their vulnerabilities and make changes where required. We explored ways to cope with boundary violations and what to do when agreements break down.

- Chapter 7 looks at building trust and the importance of maintaining that trust. We covered what causes trust to break down and tools we can utilize to repair damaged trust.

- Chapter 8 explored the predicaments associated with New Relationship Energy and managing the conflicting emotions of the early stages while keeping the lines of communication open and honest. We focused on the need for integrity and understanding during transitions.

- Chapter 9 discussed the benefits of challenging societal norms and using non-monogamy as a path to personal growth. We looked at the rewards of stepping out of your comfort zone, understanding that love comes in many forms, and experiencing the happiness and fulfillment that come from growth and authenticity.

This is only the start of your incredible journey into a non-monogamous life. Use it as a stepping stone to launch yourself into this brave new world. Take what you have learned, go forth, and have fun! Continue your education by listening to podcasts, joining support groups, reading further resources, and joining non-monogamous communities. You may be pleasantly surprised by the help networks and resources out there, which are constantly expanding.

To support you on your path to confidently transitioning to non-monogamy and having healthier relationships, please join our email list so that you can stay informed about the latest books on the subject and receive emails offering additional support, guidance, and encouragement at (https://www.infinitecreationsinc.com/).

Suppose you are further along in your journey into non-monogamy. In that case, you can have a go at implementing some of the communication strategies and boundary-setting techniques we have explored in the book. Perhaps there are things you hadn't thought to include in your agreement that will inspire you to rethink your own personal boundaries or prompt conversations with your partner to make the transition process more straightforward.

Finally, we want to reassure you that the journey you are taking will be a positive one. Taking the first steps on the road to non-monogamy requires courage and patience, but through the fear comes a tremendous sense of liberation. Non-monogamy is an adventure that will enrich your life and offer you freedoms and experiences you never thought possible. We wish you every success on your journey. May the road ahead be filled with love, fulfillment, and happiness!

Inspire Change: Leave a Transformative Review

As you conclude your exploration of "Exploring Ethical Non-Monogamy," your journey holds invaluable insights. Sharing your experience through a review can be a lifeline for those navigating the complexities of ethical non-monogamy, letting them know they are not alone.

Your review serves as a call to action, motivating others to embark on their own journeys of discovery within the realm of ethical non-monogamy. It encourages them to confront their challenges head-on and embrace the transformative power of this lifestyle.

In essence, your review isn't just a reflection; it's a gift to those seeking their own paths to understanding and growth in non-monogamous relationships. Share how the book has aided your journey, the transformations you've witnessed, and why others should embark on this path, too. Highlight specific tools or insights that resonated with you.

Your review isn't mere words; it's a catalyst for others' growth. By sharing your story and insights, you guide fellow seekers toward healthier, more fulfilling, non-monogamous relationships. Your action today can inspire countless transformations. Leave your review now and illuminate the path for others.

1. Rense, S. (2020, August 21). You definitely have friends in open relationships. *Esquire*. http://www.esquire.com/lifestyle/sex/a44853/why-open-relationship/

2. Silverstein, J., & Kegu, J. (2019, October 30). Polyamory and non-monogamous relationships are more common than you'd think – CBSN Originals. *CBS News*. https://www.cbsnews.com/news/polyamory-relationships-how-common-is-non-monogamy-cbsn-originals/

3. Statista. (2023, June 2). Average children per family U.S. 2022. https://www.statista.com/statistics/718084/average-number-of-own-children-per-family/

4. Statista. (2023, June 2). Average children per family U.S. 2022. https://www.statista.com/statistics/718084/average-number-of-own-children-per-family/

5. Haupert, M., Gesselman, A. N., Moors, A. C., Fisher, H., & Garcia. (2016, April 20). Prevalence of experiences with consensual non-monogamous relationships: findings from two national samples of single Americans. Journal of Sex & Marital Therapy, 43(5), 424–440. https://doi.org/10.1080/0092623x.2016.1178675

6. Greeley, A.M. (1991). Faithful attraction. New York: Tom Doherty Associates.

7. New Realities Of Love: Is Ethical Non-Monogamy For Real? (2023, March 20). The Next Cartel. https://thenextcartel.com/observatory/new-real ities-of-love-is-ethical-non-monogamy-for-real/

8. Ryan, C., & Jetha, C. (2021). Sex at dawn: How We Mate, Why We Stray, and What It Means for Modern Sexuality.

9. Furman, W., & Shaffer, L. A. (2011). Romantic Partners, Friends, Friends with Benefits, and Casual Acquaintances as Sexual Partners. Journal of Sex Research, 48(6), 554–564. https://doi.org/10.1080/00224 499.2010.535623

10. Moors, A. C., Schechinger, H., Balzarini, R. N., & Flicker, S. M. (2021). Internalized consensual Non-Monogamy negativity and relationship quality among people engaged in polyamory, swinging, and open relationships. Archives of Sexual Behavior, 50(4), 1389–1400. https://doi.org/10.1007/s10508-020-01885-7

11. Hnatkovičová, D., & Bianchi, G. (2022). Model of motivations for engaging in polyamorous relationships. Sexologies, 31(3), 184–194. https://doi.org/10.1016/j.sexol.2022.03.003

12. Kerner, I. (2023, February 19). Can a monogamous couple happily become nonmonogamous? It's possible but not easy, experts say. CNN. https://edition.cnn.com/2023/02/19/health/couples-explore-nonmonogamous-relationships-wellness/index.html

13. Kerner, I. (2023, February 19). Can a monogamous couple happily become nonmonogamous? It's possible but not easy, experts say. CNN. https://edition.cnn.com/2023/02/19/health/couples-explore-nonmonogamous-relationships-wellness/index.html

14. Schucman, H. (2007). Chapter 22: Weakness and Defensiveness | ACIM. A Course in Miracles. V1:12. https://acim.org/acim/chapter-22/introduction/en/s/261

15. Schucman, H. (2007). Chapter 22: Weakness and Defensiveness | ACIM. A Course in Miracles. V3:10-11. https://acim.org/acim/chapter-22/weakness-and-defensiveness/en/s/266#3:10-11

16. Barker, M., & Langdridge, D. (2010). Understanding Non-Monogamies. Routledge.

17. Wood, J., De Santis, C., Desmarais, S., & Milhausen, R. R. (2021). Motivations for engaging in consensually Non-Monogamous relationships. Archives of Sexual Behavior, 50(4), 1253–1272. https://doi.org/10.1007/s10508-020-01873-x

18. Balzarini, R. (2018). Understanding stigma, secrecy, and sex in CNM relationships. Electronic Thesis and Dissertation Repository. 5613. https://ir.lib.uwo.ca/etd/5613

19. Munro, S. (2017, September 15). A moment that changed me: turning my back on monogamy. The Guardian. https://www.theguardian.com/commentisfree/2017/sep/15/moment-that-changed-me-monogamy-polyamory-jealousy

20. Gonsalves, K. (2022, October 31). Why So Many People Are Interested In Ethical Non-Monogamy These Days. Mindbodygreen. https://www.mindbodygreen.com/articles/ethical-non-monogamy-guide#

21. Aubrey Marcus. (2018, May 2). Lessons On Jealousy From an Open Relationship. https://www.aubreymarcus.com/blogs/aubrey-marcus/jealousy

22. Aubrey Marcus. (2018, May 2). Lessons On Jealousy From an Open Relationship. https://www.aubreymarcus.com/blogs/aubrey-marcus/jealousy

23. Munro, S. (2017, September 15). A moment that changed me: turning my back on monogamy. The Guardian. https://www.theguardian.com/commentisfree/2017/sep/15/moment-that-changed-me-monogamy-polyamory-jealousy

24. Taormino, T. (2008). Opening up: A Guide To Creating and Sustaining Open Relationships. Cleis Press.

25. Aubrey Marcus. (2018, May 2). Lessons On Jealousy From an Open Relationship. https://www.aubreym arcus.com/blogs/aubrey-marcus/jealousy

26. Anderson, E. H., & Shivakumar, G. (2013, April 23). Effects of exercise and physical activity on anxiety. Frontiers in Psychiatry, 4. https://doi.org/10.3389/fpsyt.2013.00027

27. Katie, B., & Mitchell, S. (2008). Loving what is: Four Questions That Can Change Your Life. Random House.

28. Abke, A. (2023, June 22). The Law of One Method | RA's practice of catalyst Integration [Video]. YouTube. Retrieved August 9, 2023. https://www.youtube.com/watch?v=KnXQ6-tqWQk

29. Smith, S. (2018, April 10). 5-4-3-2-1 coping technique for anxiety. https://www.urmc.rochester.edu/behavioral-health -partners/bhp-blog/april-2018/5-4-3-2-1-coping-tec hnique-for-anxiety.aspx

30. LePera, N. (2021). How To Do The Work: The Sunday Times Bestseller. Hachette UK.

31. Van Der Kolk, B. (2014). The body keeps the score: Mind, Brain and Body in the Transformation of Trauma. Penguin UK.

32. Stavros, C. (2023). Therapies to reset your whole body nervous system - Advanced Musculoskeletal Medicine Consultants, Inc. Advanced Musculoskeletal Medicine Consultants, Inc. https://advancedmmc.com/therapies-to-reset-your-nervous-system/

33. Lowen Foundation. What is Bioenergetics? (n.d.). Lowen Foundation. https://www.lowenfoundation.org/what-is-bioenergetics

34. Stavros, C. (2023). Therapies to reset your whole body nervous system - Advanced Musculoskeletal Medicine Consultants, Inc. Advanced Musculoskeletal Medicine Consultants, Inc. https://advancedmmc.com/therapies-to-reset-your-nervous-system/

35. Kelloway. L. (2023). 5 Somatic experiencing techniques that anyone can use to stay grounded. Life Care Wellness. https://life-care-wellness.com/5-somatic-experiencing-techniques-that-anyone-can-use-to-stay-grounded/

36. Sutton, J., PhD. (2023). 7 Stress-Relief breathing exercises for calming your mind. PositivePsychology.com. https://positivepsychology.com/breathing-exercises-for-stress-relief/

37. Freund, M. (2023, May 30). Can you reset your own nervous system? Ness. https://ness-well.com/how-to-reset-your-nervous-system/

38. Ross, P. (2020). 5 herbs to support your stress response & nervous system. Richmond Natural Medicine. https://richmondnaturalmed.com/5-herbs-to-support-your-stress-response-nervous-system/

39. Dana, D. A., & Porges, S. W. (2018). Polyvagal Theory in therapy: Engaging the Rhythm of Regulation. National Geographic Books.

40. Jahromi, V. K., Tabatabaee, S. S., Abdar, Z. E., & Rajabi, M. (2016). Active listening: The key of successful communication in hospital managers. Electronic Physician, 8(3), 2123–2128. https://doi.org/10.19082/2123

41. Johnston, E. (2022). What are 'I feel' statements? Verywell Mind. https://www.verywellmind.com/what-are-feeling-statements-425163

42. Schultz, J. (2023). Your complete Nonviolent communication guide. PositivePsychology.com . https://positivepsychology.com/non-violent-com munication/#

43. Roter, D., Frankel, R. M., Hall, J. A., & Sluyter, D. (2006). The expression of emotion through nonverbal behavior in medical visits. Mechanisms and outcomes. Journal of General Internal Medicine, 21(S1), S28–S34. https://doi.org/10.1111/j.1525-1497.2006.00306.x

44. Segal, J. Ph.D.. (2023). Emotional intelligence in love and relationships. HelpGuide.org . https://www.helpguide.org/articles/mental-health/ emotional-intelligence-love-relationships.htm

45. Gottman Institute. (2019, August 26). Marriage and Couples - Research | The Gottman Institute. https://www.gottman.com/about/research/couples/

46. Braithwaite, S. R., Selby, E. A., & Fincham, F. D. (2011). Forgiveness and relationship satisfaction: Mediating mechanisms. Journal of Family Psychology, 25(4), 551–559. https://doi.org/10.1037/a0024526

47. Cloud, H., & Townsend, J. (1992). Boundaries: When to Say Yes, When to Say No To Take Control of Your Life. Zondervan.

48. Borst, H. (2023, January 31). The 5
    Love Languages—And How To Use Them
    To Strengthen Your Relationship. Forbes
    Health. https://www.forbes.com/health/mind/what
    -are-the-five-love-languages/

49. Fuller, C., and J. (2022). Broken trust and polyamory.
    Touch of Flavor. https://atouchofflavor.com/broken
    -trust-and-polyamory/

50. Williams, F. (2021, November 9). 5 Tips for a Smooth
    Transition into Ethical Non-Monogamy. The
    Human Condition.
    https://www.thehumanconditioncoaching.com/post/
    setting-a-container-for-a-smooth-transition-into-e
    thical-non-monogamy

51. Fleckenstein, J. R., & Cox, D. W. (2014). The associa-
    tion of an open relationship orientation with health
    and happiness in a sample of older US adults. Sexual
    and Relationship Therapy, 30(1), 94–116. https://doi
    .org/10.1080/14681994.2014.976997

52. McGahan, M. (2023, May 10). Non-Monogamous celebs: Will Smith, Jada Pinkett Smith and more. Us Weekly. https://www.usmagazine.com/celebrity-news/pictur es/non-monogamous-celebs-will-smith-jada-pinket t-smith-and-more/#

53. Brenner, A. M.D.. (2015, December 27). 5 Benefits of Stepping Outside Your Comfort Zone. Psychology Today. https://www.psychologyto- day.com/us/blog/in-flux/201512/5-benefits-step- ping-outside-your-comfort-zone

54. Cherry, K. (2023, May 2). Emotional intelligence: how we perceive, evaluate, express, and control emotions. Verywell Mind. https://www.verywellmin d.com/what-is-emotional-intelligence-2795423

55. Alabi, O. (2023, April 3). How To Improve Your Emotional Intelligence: 4 Steps To Boost Your EQ. Forbes. https://www.forbes.com/sites/forbesbusinesscouncil /2023/04/03/how-to-improve-your-emotional-intelli gence-4-steps-to-boost-your-eq/

56. Segal, J. Ph.D.. (2023). Emotional intelligence in love and relationships. HelpGuide.org . https://www.helpguide.org/articles/mental-health/emotional-intelligence-love-relationships.htm

57. Naiman, M. (2017, July 18). Authenticity is the Cornerstone of Personal Growth. www.linkedin.com . https://www.linkedin.com/pulse/authenticity-cornerstone-personal-growth-miranda-zelda-naiman/

58. Sinclair, L. (2022, May 29). A Journey To Authenticity Through Non Monogamy. Medium. https://hello-lizsinclair.medium.com/a-journey-to-authenticity-through-non-monogamy-476152de0d54

59. O'Sullivan, O. (2023, April 5). 7 Astonishing Ways That Conflict Helps You Grow In Non-Monogamy. https://blog.hashtagopen.com/7-ways-conflict-helps-grow-non-monogamy/

60. BBC News. (2014, June 24). How Kenyans are reacting to legalised polygamy. BBC News. https://www.bbc.com/news/world-africa-27939037

61. Cohn, C. L. (2014). A Visual Guide To Non-Monogamy Around the World. Matador Network. https://matadornetwork.com/life/non-monogamy-around-world/

62. Xin, C. (2023, June 10). Polyandry families in Tibet. Tibet Travel and Tours - Tibet Vista. https://www.tibettravel.org/tibetan-people/polyandry-in-tibet.html

www.ingramcontent.com/pod-product-compliance
Lightning Source LLC
Chambersburg PA
CBHW071414150726
48000CB00001B/325